AN INTELLIGENT BASED SYSTEM
FOR DETECTING AND COMBATING
IN COMPUTER NETWORK

by
AMRITA

ACKNOWLEDGMENTS

Firstly, I would like to express my sincere gratitude to my first mentor Late Prof. (Dr.) Pervez Ahmed for the continuous support during my research work, for his patience, motivation, and immense knowledge. I am grateful to him for enlightening me the first glance of research. His guidance helped me in all the time of research. I could not have imagined having a better mentor for my research work.

I would also like to express uttermost gratitude to my supervisor Prof. (Dr.) Shri Kant for his guidance, advice and effort, which have been essential at all stages of my research work and shaped the thesis. I am extremely grateful to him for his valuable guidance, scholarly inputs and consistent encouragement I received for the research work. This feat was possible only because of the support provided by him. I consider it as a great opportunity to do my research work under his guidance and to learn from his research expertise.

Also I am extremely grateful to Dr. Kiran Kumar Ravulakollu for his insightful advice, encouragement, comments, discussions, and guidance during this research work. His constant guidance, cooperation, and support have always kept me going ahead.

Besides, I also express my sincere gratitude and honor to my institute Sharda University, Greater Noida. I express my gratitude to HoD (CSE), Dean (SET), Dean (Research), Co-ordinator (Ph. D. Program), Honorable Vice Chancellor, and Honorable Chancellor, Sharda University for providing all the academic support and the facilities to carry out the research work at the Institute. I am also grateful to all teaching staffs, non-teaching staffs, technical staff and friends for their support during my research work.

I expresses my regards and thanks to Dr. Rajesh Kumar and Dr. N. B. Singh and the members of the Research and Technology Development Centre, Sharda Uni-

CONTENTS

LIST OF TABLES

LIST OF FIGURES

SYMBOLS AND ABBREVIATIONS

ACC   Accuracy

ACO   Ant Colony Optimization

ANN   Artificial Neural Network

BN   Bayesian Networks

BPNN   Back Propagation Neural Network

CFS   Correlation-based Feature Selection

CON   Consistency-based Feature Selection

DARPA   Defense Advanced Research Projects Agency

DoS   Denial of Service

DR   Detection Rate

DT   Decision Tree

ERR   Error Rate

F1-S   F1-Score

FAR   False Alarm Rate

FN   False Negative

FNR   False Negative Rate

FP   False Positive

FPR   False Positive Rate

GA   Genetic Algorithm

GM   Geometric Mean

GR   Gain Ratio

HEIC   Heterogeneous Ensemble of Intelligent Classifiers

HyFSA   Hybrid Feature Selection Approach

HySCBA   Hybrid Sampling Class Balancer Algorithm

ID   Intrusion Detection

IDPS   Intrusion Detection and Prevention System

IDS   Intrusion Detection System

IG   Information Gain

IoT   Internet of Things

IPS   Intrusion Prevention System

KDD   Knowledge Discovery and Data Mining

k-NN   k-Nearest Neighbors

LSSVM   Least Square Support Vector Machine

NB   Naïve Bayes

NID   Network Intrusion Detection

NIDS   Network Intrusion Detection System

NIDPS   Network Intrusion Detection and Prevention System

NN   Neural Network

OVO   One-Vs-One

OVR   One-Vs-Rest

PCA   Principal Component Analysis

PRC   Precision-Recall Curves

PRE   Precision

PSO	Particle Swarm Optimization
R2L	Remote to Local
RBF	Radial Basis Function
RIPPER	Repeated Incremental Pruning to Produce Error Reduction
RMSE	Root Mean Squared Error
ROC	Receiver Operating Characteristic
RF	Random Forest
SGD	Stochastic Gradient Descent
SMOTE	Synthetic Minority Over-sampling Technique
SVM	Support Vector Machine
TBM	Time taken to Build the Model
TN	True Negative
TNR	True Negative Rate
TP	True Positive
TPR	True Positive Rate
TTM	Time taken to Test the Model
U2R	User to Root

CHAPTER 1

INTRODUCTION

1.1 OVERVIEW

Internet has grown rapidly due to growth of computer technology, computer networks and network communication technology during the recent decades. Rapid increase and tremendous growth in computer network and Internet communication has increased the growth of security threats for computer networks (Kruegel et al., 2004). Everyday new vulnerabilities are exposed and attacks are occurred frequently in Internet. It makes the computer networks environment insecure and more vulnerable day by day (Ehlert et al., 2010). These threats and vulnerabilities can interrupt and influences the performance of personal, social, government and organizational operations and functions (Olusola et al., 2013). Due to this, security of computer networks has become an important issue and essential component in modern computer systems (Singh, 2004). Network security threat can take place from external intruders as well as internal users in the form of anomalous behavior and misuse (Anderson, 1980). Network security is a mechanism of protection from external and internal threats in order to ensure security of network communications (Holm, 2012). It protects network environment against unauthorized access to vital information, Denial of Service (DoS) attacks, alteration and demolition of data and information, and information loss. There are various protection mechanisms available like authentication and access control mechanisms, peripheral protection mechanisms but these mechanisms are not helpful against internal intrusions. Therefore, there is an immense need for additional level of integral protection such as Network Intrusion Detection and Prevention System (NIDPS) against network intrusions. Network intrusion can arise in network traffic that emerge as normal (Kruegel et al., 2004; Gollmann, 2006). NIDPS compliments the security mechanism by attempting to detect anomalous behavior and misuse and preventing from them.

1

1.2 INTRUSION DETECTION AND PREVENTION SYSTEM

1.2.1 Introduction

The security of computer network becomes critical due to tremendous growth of Internet and network attacks in recent decades. As Internet becomes vulnerable to internal and external attack, NIDPS has emerged as an indispensable component. It combats the misuse, abuse and unauthorized use of resources of computer network. The term intrusion is defined as "an unauthorized attempt to compromise confidentiality, integrity, and availability or to violate the security mechanisms or policies of a computer or network" (Bace and Mell, 2001). Network Intrusion Detection (NID) is the course of action to monitor and analyze events occurring in a computer network for signs of intrusions and report if such suspicious activity is discovered. Network Intrusion Detection System (NIDS) is a software application or hardware system to automate the procedure of NID (Stavroulakis and Stamp, 2010). The Intrusion Detection and Prevention System (IDPS) is the system having all Intrusion Detection System (IDS) capabilities, and attempt to stop or block possible intrusive activity (Scarfone and Mell, 2010). The term Intrusion Detection (ID) is first coined by James P. Anderson (1980). Dr. Dorothy Denning (1987) proposed the first model for ID in 1987 named as Intrusion detection expert system. It provided the fundamental core to the ID development. Since then abundant literatures are presented and numerous approaches have been proposed on NIDPS. In spite of significant progress, there are still a lot of opportunities to enhance the state-of-the-art in detecting and combating network-based intrusions.

1.2.2 Classifications of intrusion detection and prevention system

IDPS can be classified into several categories based on various characteristics like monitoring environment, detection approaches, and system type as shown in Figure 1.1. IDPS can be categorized based on monitoring environment as—NIDPS and host-based IDPS. NIDPS monitors and analyzes network traffic patterns to identify suspicious activity, whereas host-based IDPS monitors and analyzes the events occurring at single computer or host to identify suspicious activity. In both systems, suspicious activities are identified while monitoring are immediately reported and provide appropriate prevention. IDPS can also be categorized based on detection approach for determining the occurrence of intrusions as—misuse-based or signature-based detection, anomaly-based or behavior-based detection, and hybrid-based detection (Scarfone and Mell, 2010). Misuse-based detection approach identifies abnormal behavior by comparing network traffic to predefined patterns or signature of known intrusions stored in database (Wu and Huang, 2010). This approach is able to detect known intrusion with high Accuracy (ACC) and fewer false positive alarms but vulnerable to new or unknown or variants of existing intrusions (Shon and Moon, 2007; Lin et al., 2012). Anomaly-based detection approach constructs the model based on normal behavior and monitor to identify deviation from the normal behavior to detect abnormal behavior (Bhuyan et al., 2014). This approach is able to detect novel as well as "zero days" intrusions but often has high False Positive Rate (FPR) (Joo et al., 2003). Hybrid-based detection approach combines anomaly-based and misuse-based detection approach. It acquires benefits of multiple techniques, while defeats the shortcoming. This research focuses on anomaly-based approach as it has capability to detect novel intrusions.

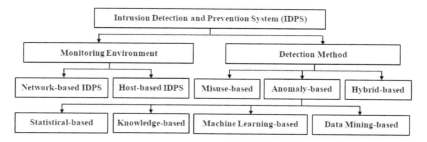

Figure 1.1: Classification of Intrusion Detection and Prevention System

Anomaly-based approach can be categorized mainly into four types as—statistical-based, knowledge-based, machine learning-based (Gao et al., 2019), and data mining-based (Lazarevic et al., 2005; Elshoush and Osman, 2011). Statistical-based anomaly detection approach employs statistical properties and test to create normal profile and use it to detect an anomalous activity. Knowledge-based anomaly detection approach defines the knowledge of specific attacks and vulnerabilities of network and detects intrusion by applying this knowledge to generate alert. The key requisite of this approach is to regularly update the knowledge of attacks. Machine learning-based anomaly detection approach constructs the model that facilitates the categorization of analyzed pattern. It constructs the model in a loop to optimize its performance and can alter the execution plan according to feedback information. It also has ability to learn and improve its performance over time. Data mining-based anomaly detection approach is best in "pattern finding" and has ability to extract useful and earlier ignored pattern from the large dataset. It also creates meaningful data for anomaly detection by reducing the amount of data stored for comparison of network activity. The existing IDS are developed using either anomaly based or misuse based ID models as stated previously.

An IDPS is a hardware or software device which has capability to detect an intrusion and can respond to detected intrusion by attempting to prevent from possible incidents (Scarfone and Mell, 2010). An IDS inspects every packet which enters into the network and generates alert on detection of intrusion. It does not take any action to prevent the intrusion. An Intrusion Prevention System (IPS) prevents the intrusive traffic from affecting the network. Whereas, IDPS detects, reports and prevents intrusion (Modi et al., 2013). Hence, it assists in early discovery of intrusions and prevents them from causing serious damage (Rao and Nayak, 2014).

1.3 LITERATURE REVIEW

This section provides a literature review related to anomaly-based NIDPS. Section 1.3.1 presents different techniques applied to anomaly-based NIDS including different feature selection approaches using single classifier. Ensemble, and hybrid classifiers for anomaly-based NIDS is provided in Section 1.3.2. Section 1.3.3 includes the area of research on feature selection and classification for multi-class imbalanced dataset. IPS is provided in Section 1.3.4. The KDD-Cup-1999 (KDD, 1999) dataset (detail in Section 2.5) is a benchmark and extensively used dataset for NIDS. It has been used for the evaluation of several research works based on NIDS. Most of the works on NIDS discussed are evaluated using KDD-Cup-1999 dataset. In the following literature survey on NIDS, wherever dataset is not mentioned, it is to be understood that KDD-Cup-1999 dataset has been employed in that work.

1.3.1 NIDS using single classifier employing feature selection approach

This section provides the state-of-art various single classifier to detect intrusion including different feature selection approaches in anomaly-based NIDS. A number of research papers regarding ID are discussed in this subsection based on single classifier used to develop IDS, feature selection approach used, number of feature selected, feature number, dataset used for experiments, evaluation metrics considered to evaluate the IDS and results reported.

The stochastic Radial Basis Function (RBF) based Neural Network (NN) output sensitivity measure is presented in (Ng et al., 2003), which is based on the feature importance ranking method using sensitivity measure. It is employed to assess the features for Normal and DoS attack only. The 8 most sensitive features {2, 23, 24, 29, 32, 33, 34, and 36} are sufficient to detect Normal and DoS. It is found that computation complexity is decreased from 23 to 9 seconds. The ACC of DoS and Normal are 99.06% and 99.77% respectively. The False Alarm Rate (FAR) for 41 features (8 features) are 0.01% (0.18%) and 0.03% (0.27%) and the FPR are 0.70% (0.93%) and 0.71% (0.94%) in training and testing respectively. A class specific detection based on Support Vector Machine (SVM) for IDS is presented in (Mukkamala and Sung, 2003). Two methods for feature ranking are applied to identify the number of important features for each of 5 classes—Normal, Probe, Remote to Local (R2L), DoS, and User to Root (U2R) as shown in Table 1.1. The system has most remarkable performance: the training time and testing time decrease for each class; the ACC decreases little for classes DoS, Probe, and R2L, and remains equal for Normal and U2R as shown in Table 1.1.

Table 1.1: Performance using all and selected features

Type	# & Features	Train Time (in sec)		Test Time (in sec)		ACC (%)	
		All	Selected	All	Selected	All	Selected
Normal	20 {1-6,10,12,17,23,24,27,28, 29,31-34,36,39}	7.66	4.58	1.26	0.78	99.55	99.55
Probe	11 {1-6,23,24,29,32,33}	49.13	40.56	2.10	1.20	99.70	99.36
DOS	11 {1,5,6,23-26,32,36,38,39}	22.87	18.93	1.92	1.00	99.25	99.16
R2L	6 {1,3,5,6,32,33}	11.54	6.79	1.02	0.72	99.78	99.72
U2R	10 {1-6,12,23,24,32,33}	3.38	1.46	1.05	0.70	99.87	99.87

A simple Genetic Algorithm (GA) using k-Nearest Neighbors (k-NN) classifier as a fitness function is utilized in (Middlemiss and Dick, 2003). Features are then ranked based on weighted feature set evolved by GA for attack classes. The selected top 5 ranked features are as DoS {1, 11, 23, 24, and 29}, Probe {2, 3, 6, 30, and 37}, R2L {3, 12, 23, 24, and 36}, and U2R {6, 17, 24, 31, and 41}. The result demonstrates that there is an increase in ACC by employing weighted feature sets. The classifiers Back Propagation Neural Network (BPNN) and SVM used to evaluate the proposed feature selection algorithm based on Davies-Bouldin Index is proposed in (Zhang et al., 2004) for 5-class (Normal, Probe, R2L, DoS, and U2R). In this, single best feature set consists of 24 features {1, 3, 4, 5, 6, 8, 10, 11, 12, 13, 23, 24, 26, 27, 28, 29, 30, 32, 33, 34, 35, 36, 38, and 39} are selected for 5-class. The ACC of classifiers BPNN and SVM employing this feature set are 0.1017 and 0.056 respectively.

BPNNs are utilized as a classifier and ReliefF Immune Clonal GA as feature selection is presented in (Zhu et al., 2005). Experimental results exhibit that it has better ACC than GA and ReliefF-GA on selected features of size 8. It has higher ACC (86.47%) than ReliefF-GA. The Least Square Support Vector Machine (LSSVM) classifier and Ant Colony Optimization (ACO) as feature selection approach are proposed in (Gao et al., 2005). The number of features selected is 9 for DoS, 11 for Probe, and 14 for U2R & R2L. The experiment exhibits that feature selection approach decreases the number of features and also boost the performance of classifier and make detection more effective in terms of time. ACC(%), FPR(%) and average detection time (ms/sample) for attack types are as DoS (95.2, 3.24, 0.031), Probe(99.4, 0.35, 0.074) and U2R & R2L(98.7,1.60, 0.078) respectively.

A combination of GA, SVM, and Correlation-based Feature Selection (CFS) is proposed in (Shazzad and Park, 2005). The Detection Rate (DR) and FPR in average are 99.56% and 37.5% using 12 selected optimal features {1, 6, 12, 14, 23, 24, 25, 31, 32, 37, 40, and 41}. The experiment shows that the DR of selected feature set is lower than full features set (the difference is around 0.83% in average). But there is decrease in training and testing time significantly though retaining the DR and FPR within acceptable range.

SVM and discriminant analysis are combined for anomaly based NIDS to identify network intrusion in (Wong and Lai, 2006). Nine features {2, 12, 23, 24, 29, 31, 32, 36, and 39} are obtained by discriminant analysis and assessed by SVM. The True Positive Rate (TPR), FPR, True Negative Rate (TNR), and False Negative Rate (FNR) of proposed method are 90.07%, 99.58%, 0.42%, and 9.93% respectively. Resilient BPNN as a classifier and normal distribution, beta distribution, chi-square analysis, and logistic regression based on ranking and feature selection approach is utilized in (Tamilarasan et al., 2006). Features are ranked based on their influence towards the final classification by using NN employing forward selection and backward elimination experiments. The selected 25 {1, 2, 3, 5, 8, 10, 12, 13, 22, 24, 25, 26, 27, 28, 29, 30, 34, 33, 35, 36, 37, 38, 39, 40, and 41} features are ranked by chi-square test. Experiments are performed to classify the network traffic patterns according to 5-class (Normal, Probe, DoS, U2R, and R2L). Experiments show that resilient BPNN exhibits high ACC and needs less training and testing time than classical NN. The overall ACC is 97.04% with FNR of 0.20% and FPR of 2.76%.

A lightweight IDS based on classic maximum entropy model is proposed in (Li et al., 2006). Chi-Square and Information Gain (IG) are used to select significant features. Experimental results show that the proposed model is effective and have good ACC especially for DoS attack with reduced testing time. The ACC(%) and testing time (in seconds) on selected 12 features {3, 5, 6, 10, 13, 23, 24, 27, 28, 37, 40, and 41} are as Normal (99.73, 0.78s), DoS (100, 1.03s), Probe (99.76, 1.25s), U2R (99.87, 0.70s), and R2L (99.75, 0.68) respectively.

Lee et al. (2007) have used minimax probability machine employing Random Forest (RF) as feature selection for DoS attack only because other attack types have very less number of records and not suitable for experiments. RF ranks features by numeric values, so top 5 important features {3, 5, 6, 23, and 29} are selected, which exhibits DR as 99.84% and 0.1039 sec for average simulation time. The experiments show that this approach is superior to the previous approaches. SVM classifier with RBF network kernel employing decision dependent correlation as feature selection method is proposed in (Fadaeieslam et al., 2007). Top 20 features {2, 3, 5, 7, 8, 9, 10, 11, 13, 14, 15, 17, 18, 22, 24, 27, 28, 36, 40, and 41} are selected by calculating mutual information and decision of each feature. The ACC of the proposed system is 93.46%. This method is compared with Principal Component Analysis (PCA) and it outperforms PCA.

A misuse detection system is proposed by (Banković et al., 2007) by investigating the possibility to enhance the DR of U2R attack. PCA and multi expression programming are employed to extract features and GA is used to implement rules to detect types of attacks. The selected features for various attacks are as 2 for U2R {14, and 33}, 3 for DoS {1, 5, and 39}, and 3 for Normal {3, 10, and 12} respectively. The experimental results demonstrate that this system performed better than the best-performed model reported in the literature. A multi-objective genetic fuzzy IDS is proposed by (Tsang et al., 2007). It is utilized to search near-optimal feature subset. The selected feature subset decreases the computational effort and enhances the performance of the system. The selected 27 features {2, 5, 6, 7, 8, 9, 11, 12, 13, 14, 17, 18, 22, 23, 25, 30, 32, 33, 34, 35, 36, 37, 38, 39, and 40} demonstrate that the proposed approach produces the lowest FAR (1.1%) and highest ACC (99.24%) with minimum number of features in the paper.

A new hybrid approach, C4.5-PCA-C4.5, is proposed in (Chen et al., 2007b), uses C4.5 as a classifier and PCA and Decision Tree (DT) (C4.5) as feature selection methods. This approach has the lowest FPR, highest TPR, fast training and testing process using only 7 important extracted features {1, 3, 4, 10, 22, 33, and 34}. Panda and Patra (2007) proposed a framework of NIDS based on Naïve Bayes (NB). The dataset is grouped into four attack types (DoS, Probe, R2L, and U2R). The classifier NB has achieved ACC of 99%, 96%, 90%, and 90% respectively on attack types, average FAR of 3%, DR of 95%, and with error rate 5%. The proposed framework performed faster (1.89 seconds) to build the model, efficient and cost effective. SVMs employing modified random mutation hill climbing feature selection method based on wrapper approach for attack classes is presented in (Chen et al., 2007a). The experiments exhibit that system has higher DR of detecting known as well as new attacks on selected features than all features with decrease in training and testing time as depicted in Table 1.2.

Table 1.2: Avg. Train and Test Time of SVM using feature selection method

Class	#Features	Selected Features	Avg. Train Time		Avg. Test Time	
			All	Selected	All	Selected
All	5	3,5,23,33,34	78	30	18	6
DOS	4	5,12,23,34	136	31	22	5
Probe	5	1,3,5,23,37	245	96	49	17
R2L	3	1, 5,6	317	24	55	7
U2R	5	1,3,6,14,33	193	78	50	15

Sheen and Rajesh (2008) proposed DT employing different feature selection methods viz. IG, Chi square, and ReliefF. Top 20 selected features are {2, 3, 4, 5, 12, 22, 23, 24, 27, 28, 30, 31, 32, 33, 34, 35, 37, 38, 40, and 41}. The experiments show that both IG and Chi square have similar performance while ReliefF has lower performance. The ACC(%) of IG, Chi Square, and ReliefF are 95.85, 95.85, and 95.64 respectively. Wang et al. (2008) utilized DT (C4.5) and Bayesian Networks (BN) as classifiers, and filter and wrapper approaches as feature selection. BN with filter based IG approach and DT with wrapper based approach are employed to select the subset of features. Ten features are selected for each attack class by using IG, BN, and DT. The empirical results show that DR and FPR of classifiers BN and DT using only 10 features remains almost the same or even better than 41 features with reduced training and testing time as shown in Table 1.3.

Table 1.3: Performance of BN and C4.5 on 41 and 10 features

Attacks	Selected Features	Methods	Using 41 Features				Using 10 Features			
			DR(%)	FPR(%)	Time(s)		DR(%)	FPR(%)	Time(s)	
					Train	Test			Train	Test
DoS	3,4,5,6,8,10,13	BN	98.73	0.08	04.7	2.1	99.88	0.00	0.8	0.6
	23,24,37	C4.5	99.96	0.15	16.3	1.2	99.87	0.14	4.6	0.5
Probe	3,4,5,6,29,30,	BN	92.89	6.08	03.1	2.8	82.93	3.06	0.5	0.4
	32,35,39,40	C4.5	82.59	0.04	14.5	1.1	82.88	0.05	1.2	0.3
R2L	1,3,5,6,12,22,	BN	92.22	0.33	02.6	1.8	89.33	0.32	0.5	0.4
	23,31,32,33	C4.5	80.29	0.02	10.5	0.8	87.34	0.01	0.5	0.2
U2R	1,2,3,5,10,13,	BN	75.86	0.29	02.6	1.8	65.5	0.12	0.4	0.4
	14,32,33,36	C4.5	24.14	0.00	09.9	0.7	24.14	0.00	0.6	0.2

Wu and Yen (2009) proposed to sample different ratios of normal data to achieve enhance ACC and to compare the efficiency of DT (C4.5) and SVM in IDS. The results of DT and SVM are compared and found that DT is better than SVM in ACC and DR, but SVM is superior in FAR. The DRs (%) of DT are as DoS (62.96), Probe (86.30), U2R (50.06), and R2L (17.43) and average FAR is 1.44%. An approach utilizing Artificial Neural Network (ANN) and SVM to detect an attack is proposed in (Tang and Cao, 2009). The DRs(%) of ANN are as DoS (59.1), Probe (82.4), U2R (65.9), and R2L (14.3) and for SVM as DoS (63.1), Probe (83.8), U2R (66.3), and R2L (14.9). The result exhibits that SVM is superior to ANN.

A "Quantitative Intrusion Intensity Assessment" approach is presented in (Lee et al., 2009), which utilizes two methods to find the value of threshold parameters. The top significant 5 features selected are {3, 6, 10, 23, and 32} by utilizing RF to detect only DoS attacks. These two methods achieve DR(%) of 97.94 and 99.37 respectively. Other attack types are not considered as they have very less number of records. An IDS utilizing fuzzy association rule mining to build stateless classifiers to classify normal and attack is proposed in (Tajbakhsh et al., 2009). The performance of their IDSs build for misuse detection and anomaly detection are compared. The IDS obtains DR (80.6%) and FPR (2.95%) for anomaly detection, compared with DR (91%) and FPR (3.34%) for misuse detection.

Xiao et al. (2009) proposed two-step feature selection approach assessed by C4.5 and SVM. The obtained 21 features {1, 3, 4, 5, 6, 8, 11, 12, 13, 23, 25, 26, 27, 28, 29, 30, 32, 33, 34, 36, and 39} demonstrate that DR and FAR increased little on selected features and the processing speed improved to 30.73%. The DR(%), processing time, and FAR(%) of obtained features (all features) are 86.30 (87.00), 15.16(21.89) sec and 1.89 (1.85) respectively. Robust artificial intelligence selection, a hybrid approach, is proposed in (Xiang et al., 2009). It is based on SVM and mutual information feature subsets selection. The training and testing times for the classifier are decreased by using reduced features and has the lowest FAR (3.49%), the highest ACC (99.01%), and DR (99.27%).

Lee and He (2009) presented two-stage entropy-based traffic profiling method to identify network attack (only DoS). Only 23 features (basic and time-based features) from KDD-Cup-1999 dataset are considered for feature selection. The top 6 selected features {5, 6, 31, 32, 36, and 37} are ranked based on ACC. The experimental results demonstrate that this method achieved lower complexity and superior TPR of 91%. A novel approach, which employed BN and two feature selection methods as consistency subset evaluator and CFS subset evaluator, is proposed in (Khor et al., 2009). The ACC(%) of proposed system for Normal, Probe, R2L, DoS, and U2R attack types using 7 selected features {3, 6, 12, 23, 32, 14, and 40} are 99.8, 89.4, 91.5, 99.9, and 69.2 respectively.

A lightweight NIDS using new hybrid feature selection approach is proposed in (Hong and Haibo, 2009). It uses enhanced C4.5 and Chi-Square approaches for feature selection. The top 5 extracted features by C4.5-Chi2 are {3, 4, 5, 8, and 25}. The experimental results demonstrate that there is significant decrease in training time (0.02 sec) and testing time (0.03 sec) while retaining high DR(%) and low FPR(%) as Normal (99.9, 1.6), Probe (93.87, 1.82), R2L (61.55, 12.17), DoS (99.3,

1.48), and U2R (50.01, 28.32) respectively. Two schemes—known detection scheme and unknown detection scheme are proposed in (Suebsing and Hiransakolwong, 2009). The known detection scheme employed DT (C5.0) with Euclidean Distance whereas the unknown detection scheme employed DT (C5.0) with Cosine Similarity to select features for known and unknown attacks respectively to construct a model. The known and unknown detection schemes extract 30 and 24 important features respectively. The TPR(%), FPR(%), and time to build model (sec) using selected features for known attack and unknown attack are (98.12, 1.87, 51) and (68.28, 31.72, 45) respectively as depicted in Table 1.4.

Table 1.4: TPR(%), FPR(%) & Build Time of known and unknown attack

Type	#Feature	Features	Overall TPR(%)	Overall FPR(%)	Build Time
Features for Known Attack	30	1,2,12,25,26,27,28,30,31,35, 37,38,39,40,41,5,6,7,8,9,10,11, 13,14,15,16,17,18,19 and 22	98.12	1.87	51
Features for Unknown Attack	24	1,2,12,25,26,27,28,30,31,35, 37,38,39,40,41,3,4,23,24,29, 32,33,34 and 36	68.28	31.72	45

An anomaly detection based random effects logistic regression model is proposed in (Mok et al., 2010), which not only considers system characteristics, but also the uncertainty that cannot be explained by such predictor characteristics. As a result, five input variables are selected as {2, 10, 12, 13, and 24}. The ACC of the proposed model on training dataset is 98.96%, while on validation data set is 98.74%. An anomaly detection based approach is proposed in (Ibrahim, 2010), which utilizes distributed time-delay ANN. The training dataset contains 25000 instances (5000 instances for each class of Normal, DoS, U2R, Probe, R2L), and testing dataset contains 2500 instances (500 instances for each type) are used. The experimental results show that overall ACC is 99.88%. The ACC(%) for all classes are as Normal (98.40), DoS (97.60), U2R (96.20), Probe (98.20), and R2L (95.80).

An automatic feature selection method using CFS, evaluated by BayesNet and DT(C4.5), is presented by (Nguyen et al., 2010). The number of features and selected features are as—for Normal&Probe are 6{5, 6, 12, 29, 37, and 41}; Normal&DoS are 3{5, 6, and 12}; Normal&R2L are 2{10 and 22}; and Normal&U2R

is 1{14}. Average ACCs(%) of BayesNet and C4.5 are 98.82 and 99.41 respectively. This method outperforms the GA-CFS and best-first-CFS methods. A novel inconsistency-based feature selection method with DT (C4.5) is proposed by (Chen et al., 2010). The proposed method is compared with CFS and it outperforms CFS as shown in Table 1.5. This method is simple and quick and can be applied for lightweight IDS.

Table 1.5: Performance of all features, proposed and CFS method

Attack	All features		Proposed Method			CFS Method		
Type	ACC (%)	Train Time(s)	# & Features	ACC (%)	Train Time(s)	# & Features	ACC (%)	Train Time(s)
All	99.50	3.72	8(1,3,5,25,32, 34,36,40)	99.45	0.48	11(2,3,4,5,6,10, 23,24,25,36,37)	99.67	6.28
DoS	99.94	1.08	4(3,4,10,23)	99.81	0.22	4(2,5,16,22)	99.32	0.33
Probe	99.85	0.66	4(3,5,35,36)	99.77	0.16	4(5,6,25,37)	94.35	0.27
R2U	98.99	0.22	5(3,5,12,32,35)	99.13	9.13	5(3,5,10,24,33)	98.05	0.11
U2R	100.0	0.11	2(3,41)	100.00	0.09	9(3,10,24,29,31, 32,33,34,40)	100.0	0.08

The features extraction based customized features to enhance the ACC of the signature detection classification model is proposed in (Othman et al., 2010). Eleven features {5, 6, 13, 23, 24, 25, 26, 33, 36, 37, and 38} are selected and experiment is carried out on three randomly selected datasets from KDD-Cup-1999 and four data mining methods DT, PART, ripple-down rule learner, and Repeated Incremental Pruning to Produce Error Reduction (RIPPER). The result shows that DRs have increased between 0.4% to 9% and FARs decreased between 0.17% to 0.5%.

BPNN is proposed in (Han et al., 2011) for IDS for the classification of normal and attack. 2570 records are selected from KDD-Cup-99 dataset, of which 1325 for training (Normal=631, Attack=694) and 1245 for testing (Normal=523, Attack=722). The experimental results are as DR (80.5%), FAR (7.4%) and FNR (11.3%). A fuzzy class-association rule mining method is presented in (Mabu et al., 2011) based on genetic network programming utilizing sub-attribute to detect intrusion for NIDS. This approach can be used for anomaly as well as misuse detection. The DR(%), FPR(%), and FNR(%) are 98.7, 0.53, and 3.75 respectively for normal or attack detection.

A method for IDS utilizing NB and an improved IG method based on feature redundancy is presented in (Xian et al., 2011). Twelve features {2, 3, 5, 6, 8, 10, 12, 23, 25, 36, 37, and 38} are selected by applying improved IG. The experiments are performed on 41 features and 12 features exhibit DR(%) of 96.19 and 96.80, processing times (in sec.) of 8.34 and 2.08, and FPR(%) of 5.22 and 1.02 respectively. A novel approach, genetic quantum Particle Swarm Optimization (PSO), is proposed in (Gong et al., 2011) to reduce features for NIDS. The result demonstrates that this method is more efficient than quantum PSO and PSO methods to eliminate redundant and independent features. DR and speed of NIDS are greatly increased by employing this method evaluated by SVM as shown in Table 1.6.

Table 1.6: Experimental results of SVM on selected and all features

Type	# & Features	Train Time(ms)		Test Time(ms)		DR(%)		Error Report Rate(%)	
		Selected	All	Selected	All	Selected	All	Selected	All
DoS	10(2,6,3,12,21,22, 31,26, 28, 30)	0.0627	0.261	0.0581	0.486	99.98	96.40	0.00	0.0013
Probe	5(5,12,26,32,34)	0.0431	0.270	0.0478	0.164	91.77	58.90	0.001	0.00
R2L	7(10,23,25,29,26, 33,35)	0.0530	0.274	0.0140	0.352	98.26	81.47	0.00	0.0016
U2R	5(2,3,17,32,36)	0.0006	0.001	0.0016	0.035	100.00	66.70	0.0003	0.0012

Hidden NB approach, which relaxes the NB's assumption of conditional independence, is proposed in (Koc et al., 2012). The feature set {3, 5, 6, 12, 23, 31, and 32} consists of 7 out of 41 features. The empirical results demonstrate that hidden NB approach achieved overall a better performance in terms of ACC, misclassification cost, and error rate compared to classical NB approach and other leading state-of-the-art models. This model has ACC of 93.73% and error rate of 6.28%. A reliable and efficient classifier is built by (Li et al., 2012) to classify a network traffic to be normal or not. It is a combination of SVM, ACO and clustering method. Nineteen critical features {2, 4, 8, 10, 14, 15, 19, 25, 27, 29, 31, 32, 33, 34, 35, 36, 37, 38, and 40} are selected by employing gradually feature removal approach. SVM achieved ACC of 98.62%, average Matthews Correlation Coefficient of 0.8612 with greatly reduced training and testing time as 04.63 and 0.12 seconds respectively.

The paper (Osama and Othman, 2012) proposed Bees Algorithm using SVM, a wrapper-based feature selection method. Bees Algorithm is used as a search strategy in wrapper method for feature subset generation. The experiments utilized four random subsets collected from KDD-Cup-1999. The result shows that the feature subset of 6 features {3, 12, 24, 25, 32, and 37} produced by Bees Algorithm-SVM has yielded ACC of 93.30% and DR of 95.75%.

A novel network anomaly detection approach is presented in (Louvieris et al., 2013). It identifies attack features to detect previously unknown attacks. The DT (C4.5) classifier, NB feature selection, and k-means clustering methods are uniquely combined by effects-based feature detection method. The ACC of the proposed approach is 99.95%. A hybrid filtering feature selection method is proposed in (Karimi et al., 2013). This approach removes useless and irrelevant features by selecting and ranking reliable features for more reliable and accurate IDS. Two filter based approaches—symmetrical uncertainty and IG are employed to create two reliable feature subsets in the first phase. Then these subsets are fused, weighted and ranked to get the significant features. The selected 4 important features for each group are as Normal-Dos= {2, 5, 23, and 36}, Normal-Probe={4, 5, 27, and 29}, Normal-U2R={10, 13, 14, and 17} and Normal-R2L ={3, 5, 10, and 33}. The DR(%) and FPR(%) are as Normal-DoS (98.8, 0.01), Normal-Probe (95.8, 0.027), Normal-U2R (99.85, 0.002), and Normal-R2L (98.72, 0.005) respectively.

A new hybrid feature selection approach is proposed by (Amrita and Ahmed, 2013) and its performance is measured by the classifiers NB and C4.5. Six features {3, 5, 6, 10, 13, and 29} are obtained by using proposed method and classifiers NB and C4.5 yield TPR(%) of 99.4 and 99.9 and FPR(%) of 0.8 and 0.2 respectively. This method outperformed standard feature selection methods and 41 features dataset on various performance metrics.

SVM as a classifier, and PCA and GA as a feature selection approach are utilized in (Ahmad et al., 2014). Genetic principal components are obtained by searching the PCA space by applying GA to obtain features subset. The proposed method achieved DR of 99.96% using 10 genetic principal components and DR of 99.94% using 12 genetic principal components. A new robust algorithm, Bees Algorithm-Membrane Computing, is proposed in (Rufai et al., 2014), to improve the Bees Algorithm for feature subset selection using SVM. The selected 10 features {2, 3,

8, 13, 20, 24, 32, 37, 39, and 40} produced very high DR of 89.11%, ACC of 95.60% and FAR of 0.4% compared to other approaches listed in the paper.

A novel multi-layer SVM model combining kernel PCA with GA for ID is presented in (Kuang et al., 2014). Kernel PCA is used to get the principal features from data. Radial basis kernel function based on Gaussian kernel function is built to cut down the training time and enhances the performance of SVM. GA is employed to choose appropriate parameters for SVM. This model exhibits DR of 94.22% and FAR of 1.03%. By comparison with other detection algorithms, the empirical results show that this model has higher ACC, better generalization and faster convergence speed compare to other detection algorithm. An IDS, LSSVM-IDS-Flexible Mutual Information based Feature Selection, is proposed in (Ambusaidi et al., (2014). Seventeen {1, 2, 3, 4, 8, 10, 11, 12, 19, 23, 24, 25, 29, 31, 32, 36, and 39} features are selected by this method. The proposed system achieved ACC of 99.79%, DR of 99.46%, and FPR of 0.13%.

The paper (Eesa et al., 2015) proposed a new feature-selection method based on the cuttlefish optimization approach and DT classifier as a judgment on the selected features. The proposed model obtains ACC of 91.99%, DR of 91.00%, FPR of 3.92% using 5 features and ACC of 73.27%, DR of 71.09%, FPR of 17.69% with 41 features. The results demonstrate that reduced feature subset provides higher DR and ACC with a lower FAR compared to 41 features. A hybrid method employing SVM and GA is proposed for ID in (Aslahi-Shahri et al., 2015). It is used to decrease the number of features. The proposed method is capable of attaining TPR of 97.3% and FPR of 1.7% using only 10 features {2, 3, 4, 8, 17, 22, 23, 31, 34, and 36}.

A method, ACO-Feature Selection-SVM, is proposed in (Wang, 2015) for NID. It combines ACO with SVM, in which ACO is used to obtain the features by means of feature weighting SVM. The experimental results show that this method can efficiently reduce the number of features as Normal=13{2, 3, 4, 7, 8, 9, 10, 15, 16, 21, 22, 23, and 25}, DoS=10{2, 3, 7, 9, 16, 20, 27, 32, 37, and 40}, Probe=9{2, 4, 9, 21, 29, 32, 33, 34, and 35}, U2R=11{2, 4, 9, 20, 31, 21, 29, 32, 33, 34, and 35}, and R2L=13{1, 2, 3, 4, 6, 7, 9, 11, 16, 20, 21, 23, and 27} with DR(%) for Normal, DoS, Probe, R2L and U2R of 99.13, 97.09, 98.46, 98.56, and 98.68 respectively. A new method based on feature average of total and each class is proposed in (Chae et al., 2015) for feature selection to build IDS. The selected features obtained by the proposed method is evaluated by DT are computationally effective and efficient. The result demonstrates that with 22 features, the system achieved the highest ACC of 99.79% in comparison with the ACC of 99.763% on full dataset and other standard feature selection methods on NSL-KDD (NSL-KDD, 2009) dataset.

A hybrid approach, mutual information-binary gravitational search algorithm, is presented in (Bostani and Sheikhan, 2015) for feature selection. MI based on filter approach is integrated into wrapper based binary gravitational search algorithm to obtain the features, which is evaluated by SVM and tested on NSL-KDD dataset. The proposed approach selects 5 features {3, 4, 5, 6, 25} and achieved higher ACC of 88.36% and DR of 86.31% and low FPR of 8.89% as compared to classical filter and wrapper based feature selection approaches. A GA based technique is proposed to detect intrusion for network in (Rastegari et al., 2015). GA is used to discover a set of simple, interval-based rulesets. The proposed system achieves ACCs(%) of 76.2 using 8 features and 9 rules; 75.9 using 15 features and 18 rules; 78.0 using 32 continuous features and 19 rules on NSL-KDD dataset.

A new IDS is proposed in (Ganapathy et al., 2015) by using layered approach based classification algorithm utilizing conditional random field for feature selection. The optimized number of features selected are as DoS=5 {23, 34, 38, 39, and 40}, Probe= 5 {1-5}, R2L=11 {1, 5, 10, 11, 12, 13, 17, 18, 19, 21, and 22}, and U2R=11{1, 5, 10, 11, 12, 13, 17, 18, 19, 21, 22} using conditional random field. The proposed system provides high ACC(%) as Probe(98.83), DoS(97.62), U2R(86.91), and R2L(32.43).

A new IDS is presented in (Balakrishnan et al., 2016), which combines an optimal feature selection algorithm based on IG Ratio and two classifiers SVM and Rule Based Classification. The optimal feature selection algorithm has selected 10 important features and achieved ACC(%) as DoS (99.25), U2R (96.00), Probe (96.16), and R2L (96.00) by SVM. ACO for feature selection and SVM as classifier for IDS have been proposed by (Mehmod and Rais, 2016). The Results reveal that TPR achieved 98.00% is significantly improved with 14 features.

The paper (Ramakrishnan and Devaraju, 2016) proposed NIDS, in which it uses three methods. First, the entropy-based feature selection is utilized to obtain significant features. Second, fuzzy rules are generated by employing fuzzy control language and finally, layered classifier is developed to identify different network attacks. The system is evaluated on 10%, Whole and Corrected dataset of KDD-Cup-99. The overall results for DR(%), Recall(%), and FPR(%) on 10% dataset are 98.49, 98.50, and 1.41; on Whole dataset are 98.65, 98.47, and 1.35; and on Corrected dataset are 99.16, 99.03, and 0.74 respectively. The DR and FPR are significantly improved for various attacks compared with various other approaches. An enhanced model to enhance ACC and overall system performance for attacks detection is proposed in (Madbouly and Barakat, 2016) for feature selection. This model selects 12 most pertinent features {1, 3, 5, 6, 10, 14, 23, 27, 33, 35, 36, and 38} and able to correctly detect traffic instances of Normal (99.97%), DoS (99.98%), Probe (99.3%), R2L (98.1%), and U2R (72.22%). The results indicate that 12 features have almost the same performance as of the 41 full features.

A new and effective framework, logarithm marginal density ratios transformed data with SVM, is proposed in (Wang et al., 2017). It is used to transform original features into better quality features to increase the detection capability of SVM. The experimental results demonstrate that it attains more robust and better performance in terms of ACC of 99.93%, DR of 99.94%, FAR of 0.10%, and training speed compared to existing other new methods. Three stages approach is proposed in (Khammassi and Krichen, 2017). At first stage, resampling is used to reduce the size of dataset. Then wrapper based GA-LR is utilized for feature selection. In the third stage, three DT classifiers C4.5, RF and NB tree are used to build model using 18 features selected by GA-LR. RF performed best with ACC of 99,90%, DR of 99.81% and FAR of 0.10%.

An approach based on RF as classifier and IG as feature selection is proposed in (Hadi, 2018). The most relevant 13 features are selected by IG on NSL-KDD dataset. The result shows the ACC of 99.33%, TPR of 99.3% and FPR of 0.1%. Spark-Chi-SVM approach for ID is proposed in (Othman et al., 2018). It utilized SVM as classifier and ChiSqSelector to select the significant features to detect normal or attack. It has high performance with decrease in training time. A survey on NIDS using machine learning and deep learning is presented in (Sultana et al., 2019). It covers tools used to develop and ongoing challenges in implementation of NIDS. A survey is also presented in (Amrita and Shri Kant, 2019) on NIDS using single machine learning approach employing feature selection methods.

1.3.2 NIDS using ensemble and hybrid classifiers employing feature selection approach

This section provides the state-of-art various ensemble and hybrid classifiers to detect intrusion including different feature selection approaches in anomaly-based NIDS. A number of research papers regarding ID are discussed in this subsection based on classifiers used to develop IDS, combiner method used in ensemble and hybrid, feature selection approach used, number of feature selected, feature number, dataset used for experiments, evaluation metrics considered to evaluate the IDS and results reported.

A combining classification approach is proposed in Borji (2007) for ID. This approach utilizes four base classifiers k-NN, ANN, DT and SVM and combines them using three combination strategies as a belief measure, Bayesian averaging, and majority voting. The proposed method is compared with single classifiers. The results demonstrate that ensemble-based approach provides more reliable results than single classifier. In particular, the belief measure combination strategy outperformed other combination methods. The DR(%) and FPR(%) are as majority voting (99.18, 1.20); Bayesian average (99.33, 1.03); and belief measure (99.68, 0.87) respectively. A hierarchical hybrid intelligent system model DT-SVM and an ensemble of SVM, DT, and hybrid DT-SVM as base classifiers are presented in (Peddabachigari et al., 2007) as two hybrid methods to model IDS. The hybrid ID model combines SVM, DT, and hybrid DT-SVM methods to maximize ACC and minimize computational complexity. The experimental results show that this model provides more accurate IDS. The ACC(%) of proposed model for Normal, DoS, Probe, U2R, and R2L are 99.70, 99.92, 100, 68.00, and 97.16 respectively.

An ensemble approach for ID is proposed in (Yan and Hao, 2007). An improved multi-objective GA is employed to select optimal feature subsets. Then the accurate and diverse base classifiers are trained on selected feature subsets to constitute ensemble ID model by using selective ensemble approach. The experimental results demonstrate that the ensemble model improved the DR and FPR on different types of attacks. It achieves DRs(%) as 98.96, 99.98, 99.95, and 98.51 and FPRs(%) as 0.38, 0.03, 0.11, and 8.91% for Probe, DoS, U2R, and R2L, respectively.

The paper (Giacinto et al., 2008) proposed an unlabeled anomaly-based NIDS

18

based on a modular ensemble. Each module in the ensemble is specialized to model a specific protocol or network service. The empirical results depict that the proposed anomaly IDS yields high attack DR of 94.38% and low FAR of 10.44%. New systematic frameworks based on RF for misuse, anomaly, and hybrid NIDS are proposed in (Zhang et al., 2008). The hybrid IDS combines misuse and anomaly detection to improve the performance of detection. The over-sampling and under-sampling approaches are applied to combat the problem of imbalanced. Top 34 features {1, 3, 4, 5, 6, 10, 11, 12, 13, 14, 16, 17, 18, 19, 22-41} are selected by RF. The overall DR and FPR of hybrid system are 94.7% and 2% respectively.

A boosted subspace probabilistic NN is proposed in (Tran et al., 2009) as a novel machine learning algorithm. It integrates a semi-parametric NN and an adaptive boosting technique. The experiments show that the proposed model outperforms other learning methods with significantly improved DR, minimal FAR and relatively small computational complexity. The DR(%) and FAR(%) for Normal, Probe, DoS, U2R, and R2L are (99.8, 3.6), (99.3, 1.1), (98.1, 0.06), (89.7, 0.03) and (48.2, 0.19) respectively. A multi-criteria mathematical programming model is presented in (Kou et al., 2009) for multi-class classification problems. The proposed model yields high ACC(%) and low FAR(%) as Normal (98.88, 0.050), DOS (99.37, 0.001), Probe (99.23, 0.045) and R2L (91.29, 0.0117).

A new hybrid method for adaptive NID using NB and DT (ID3) classifiers is proposed in (Farid et al., 2010). The proposed method minimizes FPR and maximizes balance DR for the 5-class (Normal, R2L, DoS, Probe, and U2R). The DR(%) and FPR(%) are Normal (99.84, 0.05), R2L (99.35, 6.22), DoS (99.76, 0.03), Probe (99.75, 0.28), and U2R (99.47, 0.10) using 19 features.

A new learning algorithm using boosting and NB classifier is introduced in (Farid et al., 2011) for adaptive ID. It combines series of classifiers using vote of each individual classifier to classify known or unknown example. The empirical results show that the proposed algorithm achieved high DR and low FPR for different network intrusions types. The DR(%) and FAR(%) for Normal, DoS, Probe, U2R, and R2L are (100.0, 0.03), (100.0, 0.03), (99.95, 0.36), (99.67, 0.10), and (99.58, 6.71) respectively.

A simple and efficient real-time IDS is proposed in (Sangkatsanee et al., 2011). The

12 essential features are identified by employing IG as feature selection method. Various machine learning techniques—DT, BPNN, RIPPER, BN, RBF-NN, and NB are used to design IDS. The total DRs(%) for Normal, Probe, and DoS are 99.43, 98.73, and 99.17 respectively. A hybrid classifier is proposed in (Xu et al., 2011) to improve the ACC of classification problem in ID. It consists of three modules—Kernel PCA, RBF and PSO. The kernel PCA module is utilized to select the feature subset, RBF module is utilized as classification module and PSO module is employed to optimize the parameters of RBF-NN. The proposed hybrid method has significantly improved the DR (98.954%). The DR(%) and FPR(%) of Normal, DoS, R2L, U2L, and Probe are (94.14, 1.28), (100, 0), (81.6, 0.45), (42, 30.3) and (48, 30) respectively.

A lightweight IDS utilizing neurotree is presented in (Sindhu et al., 2012) for multi-class classification to detect intrusions in networks. A wrapper based feature selection approach is employed, which reduces classifiers' computational complexity with great impact. The number of extracted features by this method are 16 {2, 3, 4, 5, 6, 8, 10, 12, 24, 25, 29, 35, 36, 37, 38, and 40}. The proposed method achieved DR of 98.4% which is superior to other methods like C4.5, Decision Stump, NB, RF, Representative Tree, and Random Tree. A new hybrid classification method using a RBF and SVM is proposed in (Govindarajan and Chandrasekaran, 2012). The hybrid classifier is trained on training dataset which is created by applying resampling on NSL-KDD dataset. The results of the classifiers are combined using voting. The ACC achieved is 85.19%.

An intelligent algorithm with decision rules and feature selection is proposed in (Lin et al., 2012) for anomaly-based ID. SVM and simulated annealing are employed to obtain the best features and DT and simulated annealing to obtain decision rules for new attacks. The ACC of the proposed method is 99.96% and it outperforms other methods with the minimal 23 selected features. A new hybrid IDS is proposed in (Chung and Wahid, 2012). It uses simplified swarm optimization for intrusion classification and intelligent dynamic swarm based Rough Set for feature selection. The selected 6 most relevant features {3, 5, 6, 27, 33, and 35} achieved higher ACC of 93.3% than the classical PSO, SVM, and NB classifiers.

A hybrid approach which combines SVM and entropy of network features is presented in (Agarwal and Mittal, 2012) for anomaly based network traffic detection.

The proposed hybrid method has ACC of 97.25% and error rate of 2.75% and it outperformed single method. A novel hybrid intelligent technologies is proposed in (Panda et al., 2012), which combines the supervised or unsupervised with a classifier to make intelligent decisions to detect network intrusions. The proposed method has DR of 99.9% and error rate of 0.06% on NSL-KDD dataset.

Group method for data handling based method is proposed in (Baig et al., 2013) to detect normal and anomalous network traffic. The monolithic and ensemble-based techniques are tested on the KDD-Cup-1999 dataset. Three feature ranking techniques IG, Gain Ratio (GR), and group method for data handling are employed to rank the features. The results demonstrate that proposed method yields high DR of 98% using top 14 ranked features.

An ANN-Bayesian Net-GR technique is proposed in (Shrivas and Dewangan, 2014). It consists of ensemble of ANN and Bayesian Net and GR as feature selection method. This method is tested on KDD-Cup-1999 and NSL-KDD datasets. It yields ACC of 99.42% on KDD99 and 98.07% on NSL-KDD dataset by employing 31 {9, 26, 25, 4, 12, 39, 30, 38, 6, 29, 5, 37, 11, 3, 22, 35, 34, 14, 33, 23, 8, 10, 31, 27, 28, 32, 1, 36, 2, 41, and 40} and 35 {9, 26, 25, 4, 12, 39, 30, 38, 6, 29, 5, 37, 11, 3, 22, 35, 34, 14, 33, 23, 8, 10, 31, 27, 28, 32, 1, 36, 2, 41, 40, 17, 13, 16, and 19} features respectively. A new hybrid ID approach is presented in (Kim et al., 2014), which hierarchically integrates a misuse and an anomaly detection model. The normal training data is partitioned into smaller parts and then one-class SVM is built for anomaly detection for each part. The DT (C4.5) is used to build the misuse detection model. The proposed method has better DR for unknown and known attacks and also decreased the testing and training time on NSL-KDD dataset. The DR(%) of known and unknown attacks are 91.98 and 30.5 respectively, FPR of 1.2%, training and test time are 21.37 sec and 10.13 sec respectively.

A combination of optimal feature selection algorithm and two classifiers SVM and rule based classifier is proposed in (Senthilnayaki et al., 2014) for IDS. The proposed method achieves greater ACC and reduction in FPR and computation time. The ACC(%) of DoS, Probe, U2R, and R2L are 99.25, 96.16, 96.00, and 96.00 respectively using 25000 records. A new approach using SVM and PSO is proposed in (Saxena and Richariya, 2014). Standard PSO is utilized to obtain free parameters for SVM and binary PSO to obtain feature subset to build IDS. Eighteen features are obtained by applying IG as preprocessing step. The experimental result demonstrates that SVM-PSO yields high DR than SVM classifier. The ACC(%) of DoS, R2L, U2R, and Probe are 99.4, 98.7, 98.5, and 99.3 respectively.

The paper (Tama and Rhee, 2015) presented the ensemble of tree-based classifiers—C4.5, RF, and Classification & Regression Trees and PSO for feature selection. The results of classifiers are combined using an average probability voting rule, which gave ACC of 99.8% and FPR of 0.2% on NSL-KDD dataset. An SVM based classifier and GA based feature selection method is presented in (Senthilnayaki et al., 2015). It effectively reduces the FAR and more efficient in detecting the attacks using 10 {2, 3, 4, 5, 11, 12, 18, 22, 31, and 33} features. The ACC(%) of DoS, Probe, U2R, and R2L are 99.15, 99.08, 97.03, and 96.50 respectively. The online sequential extreme learning machine technique is proposed in (Singh et al., 2015) for ID. It utilizes beta profiling to decrease the size of dataset and alpha profiling to decrease the time complexity. An ensemble of Filtered, Consistency based and CFS methods are employed to discard the irrelevant features. The experimental results of proposed method yields ACC of 98.66%, FPR of 1.74% and a detection time of 2.43 sec on NSL-KDD dataset.

A hybrid learning approach using k-means clustering and multiple classifiers is proposed in (Farrahi and Ahmadzadeh, 2015). K-means clustering algorithm is employed to partition the data and then NB, SVM and OneR classifiers are utilized for each partition. The proposed hybrid approach has better DR, ACC and FAR with comparison to single classifiers. The DR(%) of Normal, DoS, R2L, U2R and Probe are 99.66, 99.90, 66.09, 79.16 and 94.76 respectively. An adaptive boosting using NB and a hybrid feature selection method using CFS and IG is proposed in (Wahba et al., 2015). A total of 13 {3, 4, 5, 7, 8, 10, 12, 23, 29, 30, 35, 36, and 37} features are selected by employing proposed hybrid feature selection method. An adaptive boosting using NB yields F-measure of 99.3% and FPR of 0.2% using 13 features on NSL-KDD dataset.

A new lightweight hybrid ID method is proposed in (Juanchaiyaphum et al., 2015), which combines feature selection, clustering and classification data mining techniques. The training dataset is divided according to protocol type into smaller subset. Next, dimensionality of features of each subset is reduced by eliminating the redundant and irrelevant features using feature selection method. The selected features are 15 {1, 3, 5, 6, 7, 11, 23, 24, 26, 27, 28, 36, 37, 39, and 41}. Then the training set is divided into different cluster by using k-mean method. At last, the DT (C4.5) is employed to build multiple misuse detection models for each cluster using NSL-KDD dataset. The experimental results show that the proposed method has better performance in terms of ACC (99.52%), F-Measure (99.57%), FPR (0.26%), the training and testing times of approximately 33% and 25%, respectively with comparison of conventional method.

A novel ensemble construction method is proposed in (Aburomman and Reaz, 2016a). It utilizes the weights generated by PSO to construct ensemble of classifiers. Local unimodal sampling meta-optimize method is used to obtain parameters of PSO. The experimental results demonstrate that proposed method outperformed weighted majority voting approach in term of ACC. An ensemble of two feature extraction algorithms linear discriminant analysis and PCA and ensemble of 10 SVM classifiers is proposed in (Aburomman and Reaz, 2016b). The results of SVM classifiers are combined using weighted majority voting. The ensemble of feature extraction algorithms yielded better performance than single feature extraction algorithm. Experimental results demonstrate that feature extraction enhanced discriminant analysis the DR. The DR(%) of Normal, DoS, Probe, U2R and R2L are 98.04, 96.77, 89.12, 14.29 and 04.90 respectively; overall FPR of 1.96% and FNR of 10.85%.

A combination of hybrid approach of DT, adaptive boost random tree DT algorithm and IG is presented in (Mazraeh et al., 2016). The twenty two features are selected by employing IG as feature selection method. The proposed method has ACC, average recall, average precision, average F-measure and classification error of 97.0%, 93.8%, 91.4%, 92.6% and 3.0% respectively. An effective ID framework, time varying chaos PSO, is proposed in (Bamakan et al., 2016). It is employed to set the parameter and feature selection for SVM and multiple criteria linear programming to maximize the DR, minimize the FAR and also considering the number of features. The empirical results demonstrate that the proposed method has high DR and low FAR using selected features compared to all features on NSL-KDD dataset. The seventeen features selected by time varying chaos PSO-SVM and time varying chaos PSO with multiple criteria linear programming are {2, 5, 35, 4, 14, 30, 12, 32, 33, 37, 3, 25, 10, 13, 17, 29, and 40} and {4, 35, 12, 2, 31, 33, 5, 6, 14, 23, 29, 36, 10, 15, 22, 25, and 30} respectively. The overall DR(%),

ACC(%) and FAR(%) of time varying chaos PSO-SVM and time varying chaos PSO with multiple criteria linear programming are 97.03, 97.84, 0.87 and 97.23, 96.88, 2.41 respectively.

A multi-level hybrid ID model is proposed in (Al-Yaseen et al., 2017), which uses extreme learning machine, SVM, and modified k-means algorithm to detect unknown and known attacks. A modified k-mean algorithm is employed to construct new small training datasets to overcome the class imbalanced problem of attack classes and also cut down the training time of classifiers. The proposed model yields high efficiency in attack detection with overall ACC of 95.75%, DR of 95.17% and FAR of 1.87%. The DR(%) of Normal, DoS, Probe, U2L, and R2L are 98.13, 99.54, 87.22, 21.93, and 31.39 respectively. A robust and an adaptive ID framework using hypergraph based GA to enhance the performance of the SVM is proposed in (Raman et al., 2017). Hypergraph based GA is used for the identification of the kernel parameters and optimal feature subset. The experimental results show that hypergraph based GA with SVM perform better than the existing techniques with respect to ACC, DR, FAR, and runtime analysis using NSL-KDD dataset. The ACC, DR, and FAR of proposed method are 96.72%, 97.14%, and 0.83% respectively using 35 selected features.

A new reliable hybrid method using AdaBoost and artificial bee colony algorithms is proposed in (Mazini et al., 2018) for an anomaly-based NIDS. The twenty five features are selected employing artificial bee colony method and evaluated by AdaBoost on NSL-KDD dataset. The AdaBoost meta-algorithm is employed to overcome the problem of class imbalanced problem. The empirical results demonstrate that there is enhancement in ACC of 98.90% and DR of 99.61% by employing artificial bee colony and AdaBoost meta algorithm. An intelligent lightweight NIDS is proposed in (Amrita and Ravulakollu, 2018) to detect intrusion from the incoming traffic. It hierarchically combines Hybrid Feature Selection Approach and Heterogeneous Ensemble of Intelligent Classifiers (HyFSA-HEIC). The HyFSA is employed to find the optimal number of features and then HEIC is developed using selected features. The results show that proposed system yields superior results than other ensembles and single classifiers. It has high ACC (99.91%), TPR (99.9%), PRE (99.9%), and low FPR (0.1%) using only 6 features.

A hybrid model is presented in (Aljawarneh et al., 2018). It uses IG to select the relevant features and DT, Decision Stump, AdaBoostM1, REPTree , Random Tree , Meta Pagging, AdaBoostM1, and NB classifiers to build hybrid model. The ACCs (%) for the binary class and multi-class on NSL-KDD are 99.81 and 98.56 respectively. A new hybrid feature reduction with ensemble of classifiers technique is proposed for ID in (Salo et al., 2019). The feature reduction technique combines IG and PCA and ensemble consists of SVM, k-NN, and multilayer perceptron. Experimental results show that the proposed technique outperforms single classifiers with high ACC (98.24%), DR (98.2%) and low FAR (0.017%) and computational cost using 13 features on NSL-KDD dataset.

1.3.3 Feature selection and classification for multi-class imbalanced dataset

This section provides the state-of-art various feature selection and classification in the multi-class imbalanced dataset for anomaly based NIDS. A number of research papers to this are discussed based on classifier/ technique used to develop IDS, feature selection approach used, number of features selected, feature number, imbalanced technique used, dataset used for experiments, evaluation metrics considered to evaluate the IDS and results reported.

The performance of two predictive algorithms DT and RF and two probabilistic algorithms NB and Gaussian classifier are compared in (Gharibian and Ghorbani, 2007). Three different training sets of the 10% of KDD-Cup-1999 dataset, each consists of different proportions of attack and normal data are created to measure the performance of these algorithms for attack classes (DoS, Probe, U2R and R2L). NB performed worst on DoS. NB and the Gaussian classifier performed better on R2L and U2R. DT and RF are sensitive to selected training data and do not perform well on imbalanced dataset. The DRs of these algorithms for attack classes are depicted in Table 1.7.

An ensemble of one-class classifiers based on different classifiers is proposed in (Zainal et al., 2009). The linear Genetic Programming, RF and adaptive neural fuzzy inference system are employed in the ensemble. A 2-tier hierarchical approach of Rough Set and binary PSO are constructed for class-specific feature selection process. The experimental results demonstrate an enhancement in ACC and TPR of Normal, Probe, DoS, U2R and R2L as depicted in Table 1.8.
A conditional random field and layered approach are proposed in (Gupta et al.,

Table 1.7: Performance of Gaussian, NB, DT, and RF in terms of DR

Method	DR(%)			
	DoS	Probe	U2R	R2L
Gaussian	96.7	87.3	48.6	13.6
NB	79.1	81.6	84.3	12.5
DT	97.2	73.6	28.6	09.3
RF	97.2	74.5	25.7	05.5

Table 1.8: Performance of selected features in term of ACC, FPR and RPR

Class	#Features	Selected Features	ACC(%)	FPR(%)	TPR(%)
Normal	8	12, 31, 32, 33, 35, 36, 37, 41	99.27	0.29	99.17
Probe	6	2, 3, 23, 34, 36, 40	99.88	0.00	99.14
DoS	8	5, 10, 24, 29, 33, 34, 38, 40	98.26	0.00	97.43
U2R	6	3, 4, 6, 14, 17, 22	99.96	0.00	88.00
R2L	6	3, 4, 10, 23, 33, 36	99.79	0.00	98.58

2010) to address the dual problem of efficiency and ACC. The experimental results demonstrate that proposed system employing layered conditional random field outperforms other methods such as the DT and NB. The selected feature sets, DR and FAR for DoS, Probe, R2L and U2R are depicted in Table 1.9.

Table 1.9: Performance of selected features in terms of DR and FAR

Attack Type	#Features	Selected Features	DR(%)	FAR(%)
DoS	9	1, 2, 4, 5, 23, 34, 38, 39, 40	97.40	0.07
Probe	5	1, 2 ,3 ,4, 5	98.62	0.91
R2L	14	1, 2 ,3 ,4, 5, 10, 11, 12, 13, 17, 18, 19, 21, 22	29.62	0.35
U2R	8	10, 13, 14, 16, 17, 18, 19, 21	86.33	0.05

An improved incremental SVM based on reserved set is proposed in (Yi et al., 2011) for NID. A modified kernel function U-RBF is also proposed to reduce the noise generated by feature differences. A concentric circle method is employed to select instances to form the reserved set to shorten the training time. This method achieved good performance with DR(%) of Normal (99.8), Dos (88.79), Probe (98.52), U2R (60.0) and R2L (24.34). An SVM-based NIDS with "Balanced Iterative Reducing and Clustering using Hierarchies" hierarchical clustering is proposed in (Horng et al., 2011). It is a simple feature selection method which reduced the dataset. The important features for each attack types are depicted in Table 1.10. The experiment demonstrates that the proposed system yields an overall ACC of 95.72% with a FPR of 0.7%. The ACC(%) of Normal, DoS, Probe, R2L and U2R are 99.29, 99.53, 97.55, 19.73 and 28.81 respectively.

Table 1.10: ACC of important features out of the 41 features

Type	# Features	Selected features	ACC(%)
DoS	19	2, 4, 8, 10, 14, 17, 19, 22, 24, 25, 26, 27, 28, 30, 31, 33, 34, 35, 39	99.53
Probe	19	3, 4, 12, 22, 23, 24, 25, 26, 27, 29, 30, 31, 34, 36, 37, 39, 40	97.55
U2R	24	1, 2, 3, 9, 10, 11, 12, 13, 14, 15, 17, 18, 21, 22, 25, 29, 30, 31, 32, 36, 38, 39, 40, 41	28.81
R2L	24	1, 2, 3, 4, 7, 11, 12, 15, 17, 18, 19, 22, 23, 24, 26, 27, 29, 31, 32, 34, 35, 37, 38, 40	19.73

An efficient and reliable classifier is proposed in (Li et al., 2012), which combines SVM, k-mean clustering, and ACO. K-means clustering is used to reduce the dataset. Then training dataset is selected by using ACO. Gradually feature removal method is employed to select 19 {2, 4, 8, 10, 14, 15, 19, 25, 27, 29, 31, 32, 33, 34, 35, 36, 37, 38, and 40} critical features in KDD-Cup-1999 dataset. The overall ACC and Matthews correlation coefficient achieved by proposed method are 98.6249% and 0.861161 respectively. An efficient and effective approach is introduced in (Khor et al., 2012) to deal with class imbalanced problem of attack categories. This approach is based on the training of cascaded classifiers utilizing a dichotomized of the rare and non-rare attack categories in training dataset. Two filter and eight wrapper approach are employed to obtain 10 {1, 3, 4, 5, 11, 12, 14, 17, 35, and 40} features. The empirical results demonstrated that training cascaded classifiers using the dichotomized dataset employing selected features yielded high DR on the rare categories and also on the non-rare attack categories. The DR(%) of Normal, DoS, Probe, R2L, and U2R are 97.4, 97.8, 73.3, 48.2 and 87.3 respectively.

A mutual information based feature selection method is proposed in (Ambusaidi et al., 2014). This algorithm obtains optimal features analytically for attack classes for NID. The LSSVM based IDS is created using selected features. The selected features for attack classes are depicted in Table 1.15. The evaluation results demonstrate that proposed algorithm contributes important features for LSSVM-IDS. It achieved better ACC and lower computational cost compared to other methods. The ACC(%) for Normal, DoS, Probe, U2R and R2L are 99.79, 99.86, 99.91, 99.97 and 99.92 respectively.

The weighted extreme learning machines using RBF kernel activation function is proposed in (Srimuang and Intarasothonchun, 2015) for the classification of four attack types (DoS, Probe, R2L and U2R). Trade-off constant C is adjusted to provide solution for imbalance of attack classes. The proposed method is compared with SVM+GA and extreme learning machine and found to be more effective in term of ACC(%) of R2L (93.64), Probing (96.64), DoS (99.95), and U2R (99.97). An anomaly-based multi-class SVM algorithm is proposed in (Wang et al., 2015) for ID, which utilizes PSO for parameters optimization. A feature selection approach based on SVM is also proposed to decrease the dimension of dataset. The experiments result show that multi-class SVM-PSO outperformed other three methods k-mean, Bayesian, and multi-class SVM with grid method in terms of ACC, FNR, and FPR.

A novel Rough Set κ-Helly property technique is proposed in (Raman et al., 2016) to identify features for NIDS. The optimal feature sets obtained are depicted in Table 1.11. The ACC(%) obtained by classifiers Bayes Net, RBF, best first tree, SVM, K Star, J48, and RF are 96.32, 76.58, 95.62, 96.89, 96.85, 96.25, 97.63 respectively. A computationally efficient and effective IDS is proposed in (Aghdam and Kabiri, 2016), which utilizes ACO to identify important features. The experimental results demonstrate that the proposed method outperformed previous approaches, yields higher DR with reduced number of features (Table 1.12). The overall ACC and FPR are 98.9% and 2.5% respectively by k-NN classifier.

An ID model using multi-class SVM and chi-square feature selection is proposed in (Ikram and Cherukuri, 2017). The top 31 {1, 2, 3, 4, 5, 6, 10, 11, 12, 13, 22, 23, 24, 24, 25, 26, 27, 28, 29, 30, 31, 32, 33, 34, 35, 36, 37, 38, 39, 40, and 41} features are selected for the classification of normal and four attack types using rank based chi-square feature selection method. One-Versus-All multi-class SVM is built using 31 features on NSL-KDD dataset. The proposed model achieved high ACC

Table 1.11: Selected features from Rough Set κ-Helly property technique

Attacks	# Features	Features
DoS	7	2,3,5,23,33,36,39
U2R	6	6,9,12,16,17,32
R2L	6	5,6,12,14,37,40
Probe	7	3,4,23,26,29,38,40
Normal	6	5,10,14,17,33,36

Table 1.12: Performance of selected features in terms of DR

Attacks	# Features	Selected features	DR(%)
Normal	5	9, 11, 23, 27, 37	97.14
DoS	4	1, 4, 14, 37	99.78
U2R	4	3, 6, 23, 25	93.51
R2L	3	23, 24, 30	99.17
Probe	8	2, 4, 10, 12, 13, 19, 30,35	74.65

(98.02%) and low FAR (0.852%) in comparison to other traditional approaches. A hybrid IDS for multi-class classification is proposed in (Saleh et al., 2017). A Naïve Base feature selection method is employed to decrease the dimension of dataset. Overall 18 features {1, 2, 3, 4, 5, 9, 11, 20, 26, 28, 29, 30, 31, 32, 33, 35, 36, and 37} are selected by feature selection method. An optimized SVM is employed to reject the outliers. And finally prioritized k-NN classifier is utilized to detect attacks. The proposed method has high DR specifically for R2L and U2R. The DR(%) for Normal, R2L, U2R, Dos, and Probe are 95.09, 93.25, 92.02, 94.58, and 91.12 respectively.

A weighted one-against-rest SVM is proposed in (Aburomman and Reaz, 2017). In this, set of binary SVM classifiers are combined into a multi-class SVM classifier for ID. It utilizes weight coefficients to correct the classification errors of one-against-rest SVM. The proposed method is compared with one-against-one SVM and one-against-rest SVM on NSL-KDD dataset. The experiment results demonstrate that weighted one-against-rest SVM outperformed the one-against-one SVM and one-against-rest SVM approaches in terms of overall ACC. Tables 1.13 depicts the performance of weighted one-against-rest SVM in terms of TPR, TNR, FPR, FNR, PRE, and F1-S.

Table 1.13: Performance of weighted one-against-rest SVM

Class	TPR (%)	TNR (%)	FPR (%)	FNR (%)	Precision (%)	F1-S (%)
Normal	89.29	80.72	19.28	10.71	77.3	82.86
Probe	89.23	93.67	6.33	10.77	56.21	68.97
DoS	84.21	98.71	1.29	15.79	97.56	90.39
U2R	33.33	99.96	0.04	66.67	66.67	44.44
R2L	30.05	98.21	1.79	69.95	67.66	41.61

A robust and sparse "Ramp loss K-Support Vector Classification-Regression" is proposed in (Bamakan et al., 2017) for multi-class ID. The multi-class methodology is based on "K-Support Vector Classification-Regression" to overcome the limitations of traditional multi-class classification methods. The non-convex Ramp loss function is implemented to the K-Support Vector Classification-Regression to lower the outliers and noises. It makes the model more robust, reliable and sparse. Experimental results demonstrate that proposed method perform better than traditional approaches on NSL-KDD dataset. The total ACC and FAR achieved by model are 98.68% and 0.86% respectively. The DR(%) of Normal, R2L, U2R, DoS, and Probe are 99.14, 91.09, 68.75, 99.49, and 93.58 respectively. An intelligent system is proposed in (Akashdeep et al., 2017). Top 25 {1, 2, 4, 6, 8, 9, 10, 11, 12, 13, 14, 15, 19, 20, 22, 27, 31, 32, 33, 34, 37, 38, 39, 40, and 41} features are selected by combining ranks obtained from correlation and IG. The feed forward NN is trained and tested using these features. The Recall, Precision and FPR of proposed method are depicted in Table 1.14.

Table 1.14: Performance of feed forward NN on 25 selected features

Class	Normal	DoS	Probe	R2L	U2R
Recall(%)	98.8	93.8	89.8	91.9	86.6
Precision(%)	88.9	99.9	98.4	87.5	42.9
FPR(%)	0.0655	0.0004	0.0014	0.0028	0.0005

A novel IDS framework "Hybrid Multi-Level Data Mining" is proposed in (Yao et al., 2017). It contains combination of three modules—"Multi-Level Hybrid Data Engineering", "Multi-Level Hybrid Machine Learning" and "Micro Expert Modify" to detect known and unknown attacks. The ACC of DoS and R2L attacks have been greatly increased by proposed framework using feature sets proposed by (Ambusaidi et al., 2014) as shown in Table 1.15. The overall ACC is 96.70%. The DR,

Precision and F1-S of DoS, Probe, U2R and R2L are shown in Table 1.15.

Table 1.15: Experimental results of attack types

Class	# Feature	Feature ranking	DR(%)	Precision(%)	F1-S(%)
DoS	12	2,3,5,6,8,12,23,24,31,32,36,37	99.88	99.14	99.51
Probe	19	3,4,5,17,19,22,24,25,27,28,29, 30,32,33,34,35,37,40,41	86.77	80.33	83.42
U2R	23	1,2,3,4,6,7,8,12,13,14,15,16,17, 18,19,20,21,22,29,31,32,37,40	11.40	34.67	17.17
R2L	15	1,3,5,6,8,9,10,11,15,17,22,23, 24,32,33	68.74	80.10	73.98
Overall	19	2,3,5,6,9,12,17,23,24,26,29,31, 32,33,34,35,36,37,39	96.70	96.55	96.60

1.3.4 Intrusion Prevention System

This section deals with the IPS. Numerous research works are reported, here below they are discussed.

The IDPS continuously examines network traffic and if a malicious activity is identified, then report about this to system administrator for further analysis (Whitman and Mattord, 2005). IDS is ineffective without an appropriate security countermeasure. A prevention system should be incorporated with IDS to assist and discover the source of an attack (Khan et al., 2015). The performance of IDPS is stalled due to high FAR produced by it (Wu and Banzhaf, 2010). Many researchers have proposed an early detection and response mechanism (Manikopoulos, 2003; Stakhanova et al., 2007; Debar et al., 2008; Sahah and Kahtani, 2010).

The architecture of an intelligent and flexible automated response system is proposed in (Papadaki and Furnell, 2006). This system is able to adapt the decisions of response based on detected incident. In (Wasniowski, 2006), data mining based IDPS is proposed. In this, integration of multiple ID sensors are examined and integrated to minimize the number of incorrect-alarms.

A holistic approach is proposed in (Koller et al., 2008) to obtain a real-time IPS. This approach combines the merits of anomaly-based and misbehavior based detection. In this, IDPS has been made accurate, effective, and practical by providing four design principles for IPS. Analysis of contemporary information security systems is proposed in (Jotsov, 2008), which employs some novel intrusion detection and prevention methods.

A multi-layered approach to design an intelligent IDPS is presented in (Awodele et al., 2009). It consists of three layers—file analyzer, system resource and connection analyzer. It utilizes misuse and anomaly detection approaches to yield superior detection and prevention capabilities. The extensive utilization of heterogeneous security devices are used to generate huge amounts of uncontrollable and unreliable security events in computer networks. Then, a data mining based IPS is proposed in (Jie et al., 2009) to manage these security events.

A hierarchical task network planning model is presented in (Mu and Li, 2010) to prevent intrusions. In this, an associated static risk threshold is associated with every response, which is calculated by ratio of positive to negative effects. A response selection window is presented to select the most effective responses to prevent intrusion. There is no defined method to calculate the negative and positive effects of responses and also for evaluation of responses. A hybrid system is proposed in (Shabtai et al., 2010) to protect against attacks from multiple sources. It combines both host and network-based components and provides the best protective and prevention capabilities.

A trusted communication protocol based on XML is designed and implemented in (Hu et al., 2011). It is based on the correlation between ID and firewall. A data mining techniques for IDPS is proposed in (Chalak et al., 2011) to identify the type of attack on database occurs. In (Sandhu et al., 2011), the authors have identified different types of IDPS techniques in the literature.

The four different algorithms—Multilayer Perception, RBF, Voted Perception and Logistic Regression are presented in (Singh and Bansal, 2013). These classifiers are used to classify attacks and SNORT is employed to prevent from attacks to succeed in network. The characteristics, principles, common detection methodologies, types of NIDPS technologies are described in (Lawal et al., 2013). It also defines the need of the implementing IDS in the organizational environment. A concise evaluation of SNORT is presented in this paper.

An intelligent collaborative IDPS is proposed in (Patel et al., 2013) for smart grid environment. It uses fully distributed management structure supporting network to provide maximum protection for future smart grids. A generalized ID and prevention approach is proposed in (Nadeem and Howarth, 2013) for mobile ad hoc-networks. It is a combination of misuse-based approaches, anomaly-based detection, and response to intrusions. It employed predetermined static manner to responds intrusion and isolates intrusive nodes.

A hybrid approach based on ID and adaptive response mechanism is proposed in (Nadeem and Howarth, 2014). The response to intrusion is selected based on attack severity and IDS confidence and then network performance degradation is conducted. A host-based misuse detection system, the Audit Expert System, is proposed in (Shameli-Sendi et al., 2014). It consists of expert system to detect intrusions. It sends notifications, e-mails, and reports to system administrators and generates and forwards urgent notifications to mobile phones occasionally.

A combination of logging and IDPS is presented in (Kenkre et al., 2015). In this, SNORT tool is configured inline for IPS. It inspects packets and drops it if any intrusive activity is found. It also logs the dropped packet.

An "Efficient Proactive Artificial Immune System based Anomaly Detection and Prevention System" is presented in (Saurabh and Verma, 2016). It distinguishes non-self and self in quest by employing immune attributes to discover and prevent unseen and novel anomalies. A hybrid approach integrating anomaly based NIDPS and signature based NIDPS is presented in (Rizvi et al., 2016). It employs the anomaly detection approaches solely for HIDPS and signature detection approaches for the NIDPS rather than utilizing both systems for each sector. It helps to reduce the resource consumption. Options are provided to the user to ban data traffic from specific sources or quarantine threats by hybrid approach based on feedback received from the host-based NIDPS and network-based IDPS.

A complete survey of IDPSs is presented in (Anwar et al., 2017). It presents comprehensive in-depth explanation of detection of intrusions and corresponding response options for different types of network attacks. It helps network administrators to deal with different attacks with high-tech technologies.

A novel IDPS for home area networks in smart grids is presented in (Jokar and Leung, 2018). It employs machine learning for IPS and a model-based mechanism for ID. The detection module obtains and analyzes features of network to decide the state of network as normal state or not. For IPS, a set of defensive actions are defined to stop various attack types. An IDPS is designed and implemented using Software-Defined Networking in (Birkinshaw et al., 2019). It monitors the system and network for security policy violations or malicious activities and specifically defend DoS and port-scanning.

1.4 MOTIVATION

An intrusion is defined as "any set of action that is performed to compromise confidentiality, integrity or availability of a resource". The term ID is originally invented by Anderson in his technical report in 1980 (Anderson, 1980). Dr. Denning proposed first ID model in 1987 (Denning, 1987). Since then, it is continuously evolving and become an active and a well established research area. There still exist several challenges and open issues posed by NIDPS.

There is a rise of number of known and novel attacks day by day due to evolution in Internet technologies. The detection technique in NIDS is not capable of protecting networks system from novel and new attacks. Therefore, there is a need for detection technique that is capable to detect novel as well as known attacks for constructing reliable NIDS. Anomaly based IDS is a mechanism which is able to identify known as well as novel attacks but it has perceived of extensive number of false alarms (false positives (erroneous alerts) and false negatives (miss genuine attacks)) (Dhakar and Tiwari, 2013; Grill et al., 2017) and in turn deteriorate the detection ACC (Bhuyan et al., 2014; Bhuyan et al., 2016). This involves significant effort to investigate these false alarms to filter true intrusions and also may overlook the genuine attacks. The real challenge for NIDS is to handle and process high dimensional and large volume of class imbalanced data in real time to detect intrusion (Tsai et al. 2009; Zhou et al. 2010; Al-Yaseen et al., 2017; Mazini et al., 2018). This process is computationally intensive and is slow to make real-time decisions to detect intrusion. The efficiency of the NIDS heavily relies on the set of features used in classifiers to detect quick and accurate intrusion and distinction among its types (Bhuyan et al., 2014; Madbouly and Barakat, 2016; Wang et al.,

2017) in real time. Also, a class imbalanced dataset poses difficulty for classifier to efficiently identify the attacks types as it assumes equal misclassification costs and balance class distribution. And hence often yield high prediction ACC for majority class and poor prediction ACC for minority class (López et al., 2013; Branco et al., 2016; Bhuyan et al., 2016; Yao et al., 2017; Aburomman and Reaz, 2017).

A variety of IDSs are existing which try to enhance the DR and capable to identify different type of attacks. Most of the literature survey on NIDS shows different preferences with improved ACC for detecting certain classes of attacks while performing low or moderate for other classes of attacks. Also, the most of available NIDS does not provide immediate prevention approaches after detecting certain classes of attack for network administrator (Anwar et al., 2017).

The IDS can be evaluated based on many factors such as ACC, performance, timeliness, etc. However, the most important challenges and issues to design efficient IDSs are ACC, timeliness and FAR in current IDS development (Wu and Banzhaf, 2010; Sabri et al., 2011; Grill et al., 2017; Mazini et al., 2018; Amrita and Shri Kant, 2019) and protecting networks system from these attacks (Ahmed et al., 2016).

1.5 RESEARCH QUESTION

The review of the anomaly based NIDPSs have posed the following problems to be considered for further research.

Problem 1: There is a need of anomaly based NIDS, which can process large amount of network traffic in real time and can detect the intrusion with high ACC, low FPR and with less computational time.

Problem 2: Due to significant imbalance among the classes in multi-class dataset, it has been observed from the cited literature that the ID of rare classes are not properly classified. Therefore, there is a need of anomaly based NIDS, which can further able to identify the exact intrusion types once the intrusion is detected with high ACC and low FPR even in the case of class imbalanced problem in multi-class imbalanced data (specially the rare classes).

Problem 3: Many researchers have worked and proposed several techniques on IDS and gave less emphasis on prevention. Therefore, there is need of developing an efficient IDPS.

Problem 4: Selection of appropriate evaluation metrics to assess the performance and accuracy of proposed IDPS.

1.6   AIM AND OBJECTIVES

The aim of this research is **"to create a lightweight, accurate, efficient and intelligent Intrusion Detection and Prevention System for Computer Network(s) Security"**.

To achieve this aim, a number of specific objectives have been set as follows:

Objective 1: To propose an intelligent model for NIDS that is accurate (high DR and low FAR) and lightweight to detect intrusion (attack) from network traffic in real time.

Objective 2: To propose an intelligent model for NIDS that is accurate and lightweight to further identify attack types from intrusion in network traffic in real time.

Objective 3: To propose a model to combat from intrusion once it is detected.

Objective 4: To identify appropriate evaluation metrics to measure the performance of proposed model.

1.7   RESEARCH CONTRIBUTION AND NOVELTY

The work presented in this thesis proposed a complete system for anomaly based NIDPS. It consists of steps from preprocessing to final decision making in real time. The steps and proposed methods used to build the system can also be used for other applications. The main contributions of this work are as follows:

- This study presents literature review of state-of-the-art in the field of anomaly based NIDPS, ensemble approaches, feature selection approaches, and IDS for class imbalance problem.

- The proposed feature selection method Hybrid Feature Selection Approach (HyFSA) for IDS is capable of obtaining optimal number of features and maximize the ACC, minimize the FPR, training and testing time of the system in which it is being used. This method is useful in any domain in which there is a need of feature selection method. For the present work, it has been used to obtain following:

  - optimal number of features for normal and attack classification
  - different sets of optimal number of features for each type of attacks (DoS, Probe, R2L and U2R) from imbalanced multi-class dataset instead of one set of features for all attack types

- A "Heterogeneous Ensemble of Intelligent Classifiers" (HEIC) has been proposed to overcome the limitation of single classifier to detect intrusion (attack) from the incoming traffic at an early stage and further identify the type of attacks from intrusion in network traffic in real time using obtained sets of features.

- A hybrid approach using combination of under-sampling and over-sampling techniques for multi-class imbalanced dataset, Hybrid Sampling Class Balancer Algorithm (HySCBA), has been proposed to handle the class imbalance of attack types in dataset.

- After detecting exact attack types, prevention mechanism has been proposed to combat from detected intrusion.

1.8 ORGANIZATION OF THE THESIS

The remainder of the thesis is organized as follows:

Chapter 1 presents overview, introduction about IDPS, and the literature review related to anomaly-based NIDPS carried out for this research work, the motivation, research question, aim and objectives, research contributions and novelty of this thesis work and organization of the thesis. The literature review carried out on different techniques applied to anomaly-based NIDS including different feature selection approaches using single classifier, ensemble of classifiers, and hybrid approaches. The literature review also includes the area of research on feature selection and classification for multiple class imbalanced dataset and IPS.

Chapter 2 discusses in detail the foundations of the methods / topics used in this research. It includes introduction of feature selection methods, classifiers, ensemble of classifiers, and methods for combating class imbalanced problem in multi-class case. After this, the chapter proposes the system architecture design of research work for anomaly based NIDPS. Then the chapter describes the evaluation metrics used to evaluate the proposed work and datasets (KDD-Cup-1999 and NSL-KDD) used in the experiments. Further, the chapter discusses the proposed HyFSA, HEIC and HySCBA.

Chapter 3 provides the methodology for Module I (HyFSA-HEIC) for intelligent lightweight, accurate, and efficient anomaly based NIDS, which is a part of proposed NIDPS. The purpose of this module is to detect whether the incoming network traffic is normal or attack. This module hierarchically combines HyFSA and HEIC. The HyFSA will obtain the features subset and then HEIC is built on these features. The chapter presents block diagram of Module I (HyFSA-HEIC), the experimental setup, and experimental result and analysis.

Chapter 4 discusses the methodology for Module II for intelligent lightweight, accurate, and efficient anomaly based NIDS, which is a part of proposed NIDPS. The purpose of this module is to detect type of attack, once attack is detected in incoming network traffic. It serially integrates HySCBA, One-Vs-Rest (OVR) binarization technique, HyFSA and OVR multi-class classifier using HEIC for the detection of type of attacks in multi-class imbalanced dataset. The chapter presents block diagram of Module II, the experimental setup, and experimental result and analysis.

Chapter 5 concludes the thesis and discusses future scope of research.

* * * * *

CHAPTER 2

BACKGROUND AND METHODOLOGY

2.1 INTRODUCTION

This chapter first provides in detail the foundations of the methods / topics used in this research work. It includes introduction of feature selection methods, classifiers, ensemble of classifiers, and methods for combating class imbalanced problem in multi-class case. Then it proposes the methodology for proposed model for anomaly based NIDPS adopted in this research work based on the research gap identified through the literature review presented in Chapter 1. There are seven main sections to portray this chapter. The second section describes the related background used in this research work. The next section presents the overall architecture via block diagram and then three modules constitute the overall architecture. The fourth and fifth sections present performance evaluation metrics and dataset used in this research work. The sixth section is on proposed Hybrid Feature Selection Approach (HyFSA) employed to obtain the optimal feature set. The next section introduces proposed Heterogeneous Ensemble of Intelligent Classifiers (HEIC) utilized to build the accurate and efficient classifier. The eighth section is about the proposed Hybrid Sampling Class Balancer Algorithm (HySCBA) to balance the class distribution in multi-class imbalanced dataset. The summary is presented in the last section.

2.2 RELATED BACKGROUND

2.2.1 Feature selection method

Feature selection is "the selection of that minimal dimensionality feature subset of original feature set that retains the high detection accuracy as the original feature set" (Mitra et al., 2002). The feature selection methods are categorized into three types as filter (Liu and Motoda, 1998), wrapper (Kohavi and John, 1997) and hybrid method (Das, 2001) by Blum and Langley (1997). The paper (Amrita and Ahmed, 2012) presented the detail about feature selection methods and survey on these three categories and different evaluation criteria for IDS on KDD-CUP-1999 benchmark dataset. The four filter based feature selection algorithms employed in this research work are described briefly as follows:

2.2.1.1 Correlation-based feature selection

The CFS (Hall, 2000) is a filter based feature subset selection method. It calculates the merit of a feature subset A containing m feature elements by following expression.

$$Merit_A = \frac{m\overline{r_{cf}}}{\sqrt{m + m(m-1)\overline{r_{ff}}}} \tag{2.1}$$

Where, $Merit_A$ is the heuristics 'merit' of a feature subset A containing m features, $\overline{r_{ff}}$ is average feature-feature correlation and $\overline{r_{cf}}$ is average feature-class correlation.

2.2.1.2 Consistency-based feature selection

The Consistency-based Feature Selection (CON) (Dash and Liu, 2003) is a filter based feature subset selection method. This method utilizes a consistency measures to obtain the smallest set of features with consistency equal to full feature set.This consistency measures also remove redundant and irrelevant features from dataset.

2.2.1.3 Information gain based feature selection

The IG (Mitchell, 1997) is ranking based feature selection method. It calculates IG of features with respect to the class. Let S be a training set containing s number of samples with labels and m number of distinct classes. The training set contains s_i samples of class I. Then, expected information is calculated by:

$$I(S) = I(s_1, s_2, ..., s_m) = -\sum_{i=1}^{m} \frac{s_i}{s} log_2 \frac{s_i}{s} \qquad (2.2)$$

Further, let feature A with v distinct values $\{a_1, a_2, ..., a_v\}$ that divides the training set into v subsets $\{S_1, S_2, ..., S_v\}$. Let S_j is the subset which has the value a_j for feature A and contain s_{ij} samples of class i. Then, entropy of the feature A is calculated as in Eq. (2.3). IG for A can be calculated as in Eq. (2.4):

$$E(A) = \sum_{j=1}^{v} \frac{(s_{1j} + s_{2j} + ... + s_{mj})}{s} I(s_{1j}, s_{2j}, ..., s_{mj}) \qquad (2.3)$$

$$Gain(A) = I(S) - E(A) \qquad (2.4)$$

2.2.1.4 Gain ratio based feature selection

The GR (Quinlan, 1986) is feature ranking based feature selection method. GR is calculated as

$$SplitInfo_A(S) = -\sum_{i=1}^{v}(|S_i|/|S|)log_2(|S_i|/|S|) \qquad (2.5)$$

$$GR(A) = Gain(A)/SplitInfo_A(S) \qquad (2.6)$$

where S is training set split into v partitions corresponding to the v outcomes of a test on attribute A.

2.2.2 Classifiers

The supervised machine learning classifiers are employed in this research work. The term classification method, classifier, and learning algorithm are often used synonymously. The classifiers are briefly discribed as follows:

41

2.2.2.1 Naïve Bayes

The NB (Zhang, 2004) is a supervised classifier based on Bayes' theorem. It computes the posterior probability $P(c_j|\vec{x}_i)$ for each class c_j to classify an input $\vec{x}_i$ presented to i^{th} classifier and assigns the target class $c*$ with the highest posterior probability to $\vec{x}_i$ using Eq. (2.8).

$$P(c_j|\vec{x}_i) = \frac{P(\vec{x}_i|c_j)P(c_j)}{P(\vec{x}_i)} \qquad (2.7)$$

where $j = 1, 2; i = 1, ..., L$

$$c^* = arg\ max P(c_j|\vec{x}_i) \qquad (2.8)$$

where $P(c_j|\vec{x}_i), P(\vec{x}_i|c_j), P(c_j),\ and\ P(\vec{x}_i)$ are the posterior probability, likelihood, prior probability, and evidence respectively. NB classifier is highly suitable for both symbolic and numerical features for high dimensional large dataset and yields high speed and accuracy (Zhang, 2004).

2.2.2.2 Decision Tree

The DT is a supervised classifier based on tree-like structure which contains branches and nodes. Each branch is the outcome of the test, each non-terminal node is a test on an attribute and each leaf node is the class label of the input pattern. The well-known DT algorithm is C4.5 (Quinlan, 1993). It uses a splitting criterion based on the GR. It is suitable for both numerical and symbolic features for high dimensional data and able to handle missing data. DT can be constructed from the training dataset based on entropy, IG or GR for each attributes. The entropy and IG are defined by Eqs. (2.3) and (2.4) respectively and GR is defined by Eq. (2.6).

2.2.2.3 Random Forest

The RF (Breiman, 2001) is an ensemble based classifiers, which generates many un-pruned DT by inducing different bootstrap sample using random feature selection from training set. It is able to handle imbalanced and missing data and suitable for high dimensional large dataset. It uses Gini Index based impurity measures to obtain the best split to build DT defined as:

$$Gini(S) = 1 - \sum p_j^2 \tag{2.9}$$

where, p_j is the probability of class C_j in the dataset S.

2.2.2.4 Neural Network

The NN or ANN is computational method that imitates the neurons of human brain. These neurons are organized into network in different ways. They are grouped into layers as input, output and hidden layer. Most commonly used ANN is Stochastic Gradient Descent (SGD) (Bottou, 2010) for large dataset. The SGD is optimization technique developed for online learning. It is a simple and efficient and becomes popular technique to train NNs for large scale learning. SGD is an iterative on-line version of gradient descent method. It computes the gradient of a single randomly picked example (x_t, y_t) at each iteration t instead of calculating gradient of the whole training set. Let w, $l(w_t)$ and $\nabla l(w_t)$ represent the NN parameter, loss function and gradient of loss with respect to w parameter at each iteration t respectively. SGD begins with initial parameter w_0 and update it at each step t as follows:

$$w_{t+1} = w_t - \eta_t(\lambda w_t + \nabla l(w_t, x_t, y_t)) \tag{2.10}$$

where η_t is a learning rate, $\nabla l(w_t, x_t, y_t)$ is gradient computed based on single example (x_t, y_t). Mini-batch SGD updates the parameter w by using gradient of small subset S_t of size n randomly sampled from training set at each step t is computed as:

$$w_{t+1} = w_t - \eta_t(\lambda w_t + \frac{1}{n} \sum_{(x_i, y_i) \epsilon S_t} \nabla l(w_t, x_i, y_i)) \tag{2.11}$$

2.2.2.5 k-Nearest Neighbors

The k-NN (Thirumuruganathan, 2010) is supervised classifier. It is simple, lazy learning, instance-based, and non-parametric algorithm. It classifies new input by calculating the similarity between new input and each records of training set and then uses the class labels of the k nearest neighbors to assign the class of new input based on majority voting. Its performance depends on value of k.

2.2.2.6 Repeated Incremental Pruning to Produce Error Reduction

The RIPPER (Cohen, 1995) is supervised rule-based classifier. It improves the efficiency by reducing errors by applying repeated pruning, suitable for missing attributes, noisy datasets, and has faster training time. It creates concise rule-sets for each class label by searching the feature set of the training dataset. It is suitable for numerical and large dataset.

2.2.3 Ensemble of classifiers

An ensemble of classifiers combine many diverse or weak classifiers whose individual decisions are fused in some ways to produce a final output (Dietterich, 2000). The fused decisions of ensemble normally give superior performance than the single classifier (Rokach, 2010). The main aim of using ensemble is to get superior ACC by utilizing the strengths of each classifier than any of the single classifier. It reduces the possibility of misclassification made by solo classifier and also defeat the shortcoming of solo classifier. The architectures of the ensemble are mainly of two types— parallel and serial as shown in Figures 2.1 and 2.2 respectively. In parallel architecture, set of classifiers of the ensemble are trained in parallel and a single combination function is utilized to combine the decision of individual classifiers to produce the final decision, whereas in serial architecture, set of classifiers of the ensemble are trained sequentially. In this, when the primary classifier is unable to classify a given input pattern then secondary classifier is trained and so on. The construction of ensemble consists of two steps: (1) generate the base classifiers, and (2) combining the results of base classifiers.

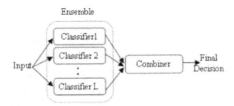

Figure 2.1: Parallel Architecture of Ensemble

Figure 2.2: Serial Architecture of Ensemble

2.2.3.1 Generating base classifiers

In the first step, single classifier i.e. base classifier of the ensemble is generated. There are two types of methods to generate the ensemble as homogeneous and heterogeneous ensemble. The ensemble can be generated by using any method from (i) different set of input training parameters available with a single classifier, (ii) different subset of training data with same classifier, (iii) multi-class specialized systems, (iv) different feature sets, (v) manipulation of output labels, (vi) Stacked generalization or meta-learning, or (vii) Voting or fixed-rule aggregation.

2.2.3.2 Combining classifiers

The second step utilizes the method to combine the decision of the classifiers. The classifier selection and classifier fusion (Kuncheva, 2004) are mainly two methods to combine the decisions of individual classifiers. The classifier selection method selects a single classifier to yield the final output for a new instance while classifier fusion method combines the outputs of all classifiers. The various combination methods have been presented in (Kuncheva, 2004) as majority voting, weighted majority voting, NB combination, Behavior Knowledge Space Method, Bayesian Combination, Probabilistic approximation, Decision Templates, Singular value decomposition, Dempster–Shafer Combination, Bagging, Boosting, Stacking, and Elementary Combiners.

Elementary combiner: Among above mentioned combination methods, most commonly used method based on algebraic combination rules is elementary combiners. This method fuses the outputs of classifiers that can be presented as a posteriori probability. The main benefit of using this method is its simplicity and it does not require any training. It contains numerous methods as *Sum, Average, Product, Minimum, Maximum, and Majority Voting* rules. These methods combine the decision of the classifiers on measurement level.

Let $\{D_1, D_2, ...D_L\}$ be the set of L individual classifiers and $\{c_1, c_2, ..., c_m\}$ be the set of m class labels. The combiner method fuses the outputs of all D_i to produce the final class label for the input $\vec{x}_i$. The outputs of all D_i can be viewed as a posteriori probabilities defined in Eq. (2.7). Let input $\vec{x}_i$ is finally assigned to class c, where c is one of the m possible classes. The *Sum, Average, Product, Minimum, Maximum, and Majority Voting* methods can be utilized to predict c are defined as follows:

Sum rule: The sum rule in Eq. (2.12) first adds the scores of base classifiers for every class and then assigns the class label to given input with the maximum score.

$$c = max_{j=1...m} \sum_{i=1}^{L} P(c_j|\vec{x}_i) \tag{2.12}$$

Average rule: The average rule in Eq. (2.13) first finds the mean of the scores of base classifiers for every class and then assigns the class label to given input with the maximum score.

$$c = max_{j=1...m} \frac{1}{L} \sum_{i=1}^{L} P(c_j|\vec{x}_i) \tag{2.13}$$

Product rule: The product rule in Eq. (2.14) first multiplies the scores of base classifiers for every class, and then assigns the class label to given input with the maximum score.

$$c = max_{j=1...m} \prod_{i=1}^{L} P(c_j|\vec{x}_i) \tag{2.14}$$

Minimum rule: The minimum rule in Eq. (2.15) first finds the minimum of the scores of base classifiers for every class, and then assigns the class label to given input with the maximum score.

$$c = max_{j=1..m} min_{i=1..L} P(c_j|\vec{x}_i) \tag{2.15}$$

Maximum rule: The maximum rule in Eq. (2.16) first finds the maximum of the scores of base classifiers for every class, and then assigns the class label to given input with the maximum score.

$$c = max_{j=1..m} max_{i=1..L} P(c_j|\vec{x}_i) \tag{2.16}$$

Majority voting rule: Majority voting rule is obtained from the sum rule in Eq. (2.12). In the decision rule in Eq. (2.17), $\Delta_{ji} = 1$ if $P(c_j|\vec{x}_i) = max_{j=1..m} P(c_j|\vec{x}_i)$ and zero otherwise.

$$c = max_{j=1...m} \sum_{i=1}^{L} \Delta_{ji} \tag{2.17}$$

2.2.4 Class imbalanced problem

Classification is a vital task in many areas. This task becomes difficult due to high dimensional, often class imbalanced massive amount of data. These kinds of data being generated everywhere in many applications including ID (Tsai et al., 2009; Zhou et al., 2010). The dataset is said to be imbalanced if class distribution present in the data is not uniform among the classes. In this, the number of instances of one or more classes (the majority class) significantly out numbers the number of instances of another one or more classes (the minority class) (Chawla et al., 2004). Standard machine learning algorithms assume equal misclassification costs and balance class distribution and hence often yield high prediction accuracy for majority class. Minority class classification is of utmost importance. It is usually misclassified or ignored or often treated as noise and hence yield poor prediction accuracy (López et al. 2013; Branco et al., 2016).

2.2.4.1 Class imbalanced problem techniques

The techniques for addressing class imbalanced problem are mainly categorized into three types—1) balance class distributions or data level techniques, 2) features selection techniques at feature level, and 3) algorithmic techniques at classifiers level (He and Garcia, 2009; Galar et al., 2012; Loyola-González et al., 2016; Haixiang et al., 2017).

1) Balance class distribution or data level techniques: These techniques balance the class distribution in the training set in data preprocessing stage. One of the well-known techniques to balance the class distribution in preprocessing stage is Sampling-based techniques (Haixiang et al., 2017). Sampling methods are more flexible since they are not dependent on any classifier selected (López et al., 2013). Techniques based on sampling fall into three types:

i) **Under-sampling technique:** It creates balanced class distribution among the classes by eliminating samples from the majority class(es). The most important under-sampling technique based on non-heuristic method is random under-sampling method, which randomly eliminates samples from majority class(es) to balance class distribution. However, it may lead to discard vital information by eliminating important samples. Another type of technique is called informed under-sampling, which eliminate samples from majority class(es) based on statistical or heuristics knowledge.

ii) **Over-sampling technique:** It creates balanced class distribution among the classes by creating new samples/instances from the minority class(es). Random over-sampling and Synthetic Minority Over-sampling Technique (SMOTE) (Chawla et al., 2002) are two widely used techniques for over-sampling. Random over-sampling technique is based on non-heuristic method, which randomly duplicates samples to balance class distribution. However, it has two drawbacks: (i) over fitting and (ii) may introduce additional computational task. Another type of over-sampling technique based on heuristic method is SMOTE. SMOTE produces synthetic minority class samples to over-sample the minority class by interpolating several minority class samples placed together. It prevents over-fitting problem but suffer from over generalization and variance (He and Garcia, 2009).

iii) **Hybrid:** It is a combination of the under-sampling and the over-sampling techniques.

2) Features selection technique at feature level: Feature selection technique for high dimensional class imbalanced dataset is to obtain optimal number of features or feature subset for minority and majority class separately (Yin et al., 2013). It also removes irrelevant features from dataset and improves the prediction accuracy of the classifiers on class imbalance dataset.

---

3) Modifying classifier technique at classifiers level: This technique tries to create a classification algorithm to optimize the performance of classification for imbalanced data. Cost-sensitive learning techniques, One-class learning techniques, and ensemble learning techniques including ensemble pruning methods are types of this techniques (Haixiang et al., 2017).

i) Cost-sensitive learning techniques: They incorporate different misclassification costs for different classes in the process of classification. It assigns higher misclassification cost for samples of minority class with respect to samples of majority class. Cost matrices are often used to specify misclassification cost of predicting samples from one class as another. It can be decided using dataset scenarios or expert opinion in a specific domain. The purpose of this technique is to minimize the total misclassification cost.

ii) One-class learning techniques: In one-class learning techniques, the system is trained by using only the samples of target class in the absence of counter class samples. This technique accepted sample belongs to target class and reject others by creating the boundaries based on the target class concept.

iii) Ensemble learning techniques: Ensemble learning techniques (Yijing et al., 2016) is also a popular technique to combat/handle class imbalance problems. Ensemble-based or multiple classifiers techniques trained many classifiers on training dataset and their results are aggregated to produce the final decision to classifying unknown samples. Bagging (Breiman, 1996), AdaBoost (Schapire, 2003) and RF are popular examples of this technique.

2.2.4.2   Multi-class imbalanced classification

Binary classification learning has been extensively studied branch of learning for binary-class imbalanced data (Haixiang et al., 2017). In this, relation between classes is properly defined as majority and minority class. Therefore, the techniques defined in Section 2.2.4.1 can be utilized to deal with binary-class imbalanced problems. In some applications like NID has more than two classes i.e. multi-class with unbalanced class distributions. From the literature, it has been noted that multi-class classification is difficult task for classifiers as it may have significantly lower performance than binary-class classification specially for class imbalanced dataset (Fernández et al., 2013). The methods for handling binary-class imbalanced dataset are not directly applicable for multi-class imbalanced dataset. Also, techniques for multi-class imbalanced classification are not well-developed. The relations among the classes are also not clear. One class can be majority or minority or balanced with compared to rest of other classes. The techniques for addressing multi-class imbalanced problem are mainly categorized into three types (Haixiang et al., 2017):

1) **Data level techniques:** The role of data level techniques is more important for multi-class imbalanced data than binary case. Therefore, proper preprocessing and sampling techniques must be taken into account based on varying class distributions and relations among the classes to boost the multi-class performance (Haixiang et al., 2017).

2) **Multi-class decomposition:** There is one well-known method to handle multi-class imbalanced dataset, which decomposes multi-class classification task into several binary-class classification subtasks known as class binarization technique (Fernández et al., 2013). Then the decisions of each binary-class classifier are combined to get the final decision. The methods defined for handling binary-class imbalanced dataset are directly applicable to these binary-class imbalanced datasets (Fernández et al., 2013). One-Vs-One (OVO) (Hüllermeier and Vander-looy, 2010) and a OVR (Rifkin and Klautau, 2004) are two most popular techniques for binarization in the literature. OVR decomposes m-class classification task into m binary-class classification subtasks. In this, m binary classifiers are constructed by using the records of ith class as positive class records and records of rest of the classes as negative class records. Whereas, OVO decomposes m-class classification task into $m(m-1)/2$ binary-class classification subtasks, where each subtask is a pair of distinct classes $< j, k >$, where $j, k = 1, .., m$ and $j < k$. The binary classifier for each $< j, k >$ is constructed by using the records of classes j and k, whereas records of rest of classes are ignored. Then decisions of these classifiers are combined to predict the output class.

OVR is the popular approach due to its simplicity as it needs less number of decomposition than OVO and employ a direct mechanism to aggregate the output of the base classifiers. Whole training dataset is used in learning phase of the classifiers in which connection records from the single class are considered as positive class and rest other connection records as negative class. Therefore, it provides robust output confidence degree.

3) Multi-class classifier: Multi-class classifier is another technique to handle multi-class imbalanced dataset problems by using modifying classifier technique at classifiers level defined in Section 2.2.4.1 without referring data level sampling and binarization techniques.

2.3 PROPOSED METHODOLOGY

2.3.1 Architecture of proposed anomaly based NIDPS

The overall architecture of proposed anomaly based NIDPS is depicted in Figure 2.3. It consists of three modules—(i) Module I: Methodology for NIDS to detect normal or attack traffic, (ii) Module II: Methodology for NIDS to detect specific attack type, and (iii) Module III: Methodology for IPS to prevent from identified attack traffic.

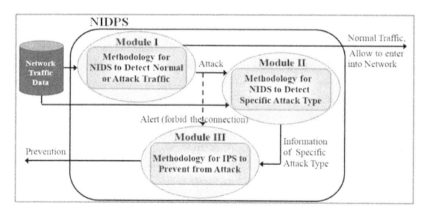

Figure 2.3: The Architecture of proposed anomaly based NIDPS

The network traffic is entered into Module I, which aims to detect whether the incoming traffic is normal or attack. For normal traffic, it is allowed to enter into network without further processing. Whereas, for detected attack traffic, it generates alert / alarm to Module III to forbid this network traffic and invokes the Module II. Module II identifies the specific attack type (DoS, Probe, R2L or U2R) from detected attack traffic at Module I and provides this information to Module

51

III. Module III is used to prevent the network by using the information of specific attack type provided by Module II. The details of these modules are described in the subsequent subsections.

2.3.2 Module I: Methodology for NIDS to detect normal or attack traffic

The Module I of proposed anomaly based NIDPS named as Hybrid Feature Selection Approach-Heterogeneous Ensemble of Intelligent Classifiers (HyFSA-HEIC) is employed to detect whether the incoming network traffic is attack or normal. It is proposed to create system lightweight and increase the performance in terms of increased ACC and decreased FPR and FNR. It integrates HyFSA and HEIC. HyFSA proposed in Section 2.6 has been used for the selection of optimal feature subset. HEIC proposed in Section 2.7 is employed to increase the performance of NIDS. The block diagram of Module I (HyFSA-HEIC) is presented in Figure 2.4. It contains following 3 phases:

Phase 1: Preprocessing of dataset

Phase 2: Feature selection using HyFSA

Phase 3: Model development using HEIC

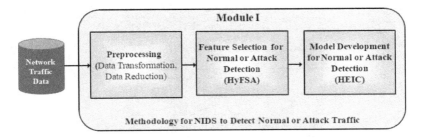

Figure 2.4: Module I: Methodology for NIDS for normal or attack detection

The detail of Module I is presented in Chapter 3.

2.3.3 Module II: Methodology for NIDS to detect specific attack type

The Module II aims to improve the ability of NIDS to further identify the type of intrusion (attack) accurately specially the rare attacks. The imbalance in network traffic data imposes poor classification for rare class data. Therefore, this module proposes an intelligent model for anomaly based NIDS that is accurate, efficient and lightweight to further identify exact type of intrusion (attack) once the intrusion is detected in network traffic. It integrates Hybrid Sampling Class Balancer Algorithm (HySCBA) proposed in Section 2.8, OVR binarization technique, HyFSA, and OVR multi-class classifier employing HEIC for the detection of type of attacks in multi-class imbalanced dataset. This combination makes the IDS system efficient, lightweight and robust to perform in real time. The block diagram of Module II is presented in Figure 2.5. It contains following 5 phases:

Phase 1: Preprocessing of dataset

Phase 2: Balance class distribution using HySCBA

Phase 3: Conversion of multi-class to binary-classes using OVR

Phase 4: Feature selection using HyFSA for each attack type

Phase 5: Model development using OVR multi-class classifier using HEIC

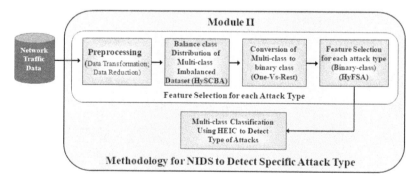

Figure 2.5: Module II: Methodology for NIDS to detect specific attack types

The detail of Module II is presented in Chapter 4.

53

2.3.4 Module III: Methodology for IPS to prevent from attack

The proposed Module III for IPS aims to take appropriate action after detecting the specific type of intrusion. The primary function of IDPS is to examine the network traffic and responds when intrusions are detected. It inspects every packet which arrives in the network for intrusion before allowing it into network. It logs information about intrusion, attempts to stop it and sends alerts to security analyst if intrusion is detected.

The proposed Module III for IPS is shown in Figure 2.6, which works as follows. If attack is detected in Module I, the information of attack is fed to Block the Packet and Alert Generator phases. The Block the Packet phase of Module III, which acts as early response to attack, blocks the intrusive packet by dropping it but does not reset the connection. This phase is optional phase. Simultaneously, the Alert Generator phase generates the alert and sends it to Security Analyst, Report Generator and Security Log phases.

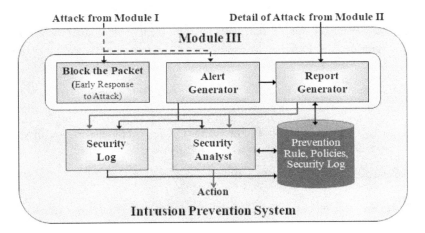

Figure 2.6: Module III: Methodology for IPS to Prevent from Attack

The detail of specific attack type from Module II is provided to Report Generator phase of Module III. The Report Generator phase generates the detail report about the detected attack and with the help of detail of specific attack type from Module II, alert received by Alert Generator, and Prevention Rules and Policies.

The Security Analyst responds to the attack as per the generated alert and report.

The types of responses can be configured according to prevention rules and policies as follows::

- Deny or Block the packet: This method is the simplest one. In this, involved IP addresses and ports are blocked by IDPS. Blocking the intrusive traffic/packet is done by automatically configuring the IDPS to "block". Hence, the intended intrusive packet is blocked at the entrance and never reaches the destination.

- Drop the packet: In this, intrusive packet is completely dropped. Once intrusion is discovered, the source is identified and the IDPS is configured automatically or by security analyst to drop the packet from the source.

- Reset connection: In this, session is reset if next packet is arrived from same intrusion source. The instruction of RESET connection is sent to the host in the trusted network. It is applicable only for TCP packets, not for UDP or ICMP. The aim is to stop the intrusion before it succeeds.

- Reconfigure firewall: In this, IDPS instructs the firewall to alter the "Access rules/policies" to refuse the packet from the intrusive source, once intrusion is detected. Hence, it prevents any attackers to succeed.

- If unauthorized user attempt or gains access to the user-name and password then user account can be disabled.

- Other rules can be defined according to the rules and policies adopted by the organization based on the detected type of attack.

The components of Module III for IPS are summarized below:

Database: It is an essential component of IDPS architecture. It is a repository for incoming packets, generated alert, generated report, stores the logs, prevention rules and policies of the organization.

Alert Generator: It generates an alert as early notification about the intrusion and then used by Report Generator and Security Analyst. The alert may take the form of e-mail messages, audible signals or pop-up windows.

Report Generator: It generates detail report about the attack which helps Security Analyst to launch further action based on the predefined prevention rules and policies of the organization. This report helps management and security analyst for further analysis.

Security Log: It helps to record about the attacks into log file, which can provide useful information about the activities for security point and for further analysis.

Prevention rules and policies: They are configured and prepared by organization for IDPS.

Security Analyst: The Security Analyst responds to the attack as per the generated alert and report.

2.4 PERFORMANCE EVALUATION METRICS

This subsection presents the performance evaluation metrics utilized to assess the performance of employed methods and proposed methodologies. There are several evaluation metrics available through which performance and effectiveness of an NIDPS can be assessed. The various evaluation metrics can be computed from confusion matrix (Wu and Banzhaf, 2010) depicted in Table 2.1, which contains detail about the actual and predicted classification results of a classifier.

Table 2.1: Confusion Matrix

Predicted Actual	Positive Class (Attack)	Negative Class (Normal)
Positive Class (Attack)	True positive (TP)	False Positive (FP)
Negative Class (Normal)	False Negative (FN)	True Negative (TN)

Following evaluation metrics can be defined to measure the performance of NIDPS derived from confusion matrix (Table 2.1).

- TP: # of attack instances classified as attack.

- FP: # of normal instances classified as attack.

- FN: # of attack instances classified as normal.

- TN: # of normal instances classified as normal.

- TNR:

$$TNR = \frac{\text{TN}}{\text{TN} + \text{FP}} \ \ or \ \ 1 - FPR \qquad (2.18)$$

- TPR or Recall or DR:

$$TPR = \frac{\text{TP}}{\text{TP} + \text{FN}} \qquad (2.19)$$

- FPR or FAR:

$$FPR = \frac{\text{FP}}{\text{FP} + \text{TN}} \ \ or \ \ 1 - TNR \qquad (2.20)$$

- FNR:

$$FNR = \frac{\text{FN}}{\text{FN} + \text{TP}} \qquad (2.21)$$

- ACC:

$$ACC = \frac{\text{TP} + \text{TN}}{\text{TP} + \text{TN} + \text{FP} + \text{FN}} \qquad (2.22)$$

- Precision (PRE):

$$PRE = \frac{\text{TP}}{\text{TP} + \text{FP}} \qquad (2.23)$$

- Geometric Mean (GM):

$$GM = \sqrt{TPR * TNR} \qquad (2.24)$$

- F1-Score (F1-S):

$$F1 - S = \frac{2 * \text{Precision} * \text{Recall}}{\text{Precision} + \text{Recall}} \qquad (2.25)$$

- Error Rate (ERR):

$$ERR = \frac{\text{FP} + \text{FN}}{\text{TP} + \text{TN} + \text{FP} + \text{FN}} \qquad (2.26)$$

- Receiver Operating Characteristics (ROC): It is a curve plotted between TPR and FPR. It is employed to measure the sensitivity of the classifiers.

- Precision-Recall Curves (PRC): It is a curve plotted between Precision and Recall.

Other evaluation metrics used in this work, which are not based on confusion matrix, are as follows:

- TBM: Time taken to Build the Model by the classifier

- TTM: Time taken to Test the Model by the classifier

- Root Mean Squared Error (RMSE):

$$RMSE = \sqrt{\frac{1}{N}\sum_{i=1}^{N}(P_i - T_i)^2} \tag{2.27}$$

where P_i is the prediction, T_i is the true value and N is the number of observations.

In general, overall ACC is most frequently used evaluation metrics for classifiers. However, this metric is not suitable for the classification of imbalanced class dataset (He and Garcia, 2009). Therefore, GM, PRE, F1-S, and PRC are adapted to measure the performance of classifier in imbalanced class problem. The GM considers class distribution equally and F1-S assess the detection performance for target class. PRC is effective useful measure when the classes are imbalanced. A high FPR deteriorate the performance of the system and high FNR make the system vulnerable to intrusions. Therefore, FPR and FNR should be minimized together with maximizing TPR and TNR.

2.5 DATASETS

This section summarizes the datasets used in this research work. The aim to select these datasets is because they are benchmark dataset for NID and helps to compare the results of proposed work with others work cited in the literature.

2.5.1 KDD-Cup-1999 dataset

The Knowledge Discovery and Data mining Cup 1999 (KDD-Cup-1999) (KDD, 1999) is the benchmark dataset for NID. It is based on the 1998 Defense Advanced Research Projects Agency (DARPA) ID Evaluation Program. DARPA'98 consists of 4 gigabytes tcpdump compressed raw (binary) data. KDD-Cup-1999 dataset is extracted from 1998 DARPA IDS Evaluation Program and it is a series of connection records. It consists of 7 weeks of network traffic for training dataset ("Whole KDD"), which contains 4,940,000 records and two weeks of test data ("Corrected Test") of 311,029. The training set contains 22 attack types and the test dataset contains same 22 attacks plus 17 new attack types (Table 2.2). Since the training dataset is too large, another 10% of KDD-Cup-1999 dataset as "10% KDD" is widely used dataset. Each record has a label of either normal or one specific attack type. The attack type falls into one of the four attacks categories as: (i) DoS, (ii) Probe, (iii) R2L, and (iv) U2R attack.

Table 2.2: Attacks in "Whole KDD" and "Corrected Test" datasets

Category	Attack Name	
	Whole KDD	Corrected Test
DoS	Back, Land, Neptune, Smurf, Pod, Teardrop	Neptune, Smurf, Pod, Teardrop, Land, Back, Apache2, Udpstorm, Processtable, MailBomb
Probe	Port-sweep, IP-sweep, Nmap, Satan	Nmap, PortSweep, IpSweep, Saint, Satan, Mscan
R2L	Ftp-write, Guess-password, Phf, Imap, Multihop, spy, warezclient, Warezmaster	Ftp-Write, Guess-Password, Phf, Imap, Multihop, spy, warezclient, Warezmaster, Xlock, Named, Worm, Send-Mail, Xsnoop, Snmpgetattack, Snmp-Guess, httptunnel.
U2R	Buffer-overflow, Perl, Load-module, Rootkit	Buffer-Overflow, Load-Module, Perl, Rootkit, Xterm, Ps, Sqlattack

These datasets ("10% KDD" & "Corrected Test") consists of duplicate records, which will affect the learning of the classifier. After eliminating the records, the datasets are reduced significantly, which consist of only unique records, are named as "Uni KDD" and "Uni Corr". Table 2.3 depicts the statistics of the records of normal and each attack type in "Whole KDD", "10% KDD", "Uni KDD", "Corrected Test" and "Uni Corr" datasets respectively. Each connection record consists of 41 features plus a label as either normal or a specific attack type. The 41 features are numbered in order as 1,2,3,......,41. There are 9 discrete (symbolic) and 32 continuous (numerical) features shown in Table 2.4.

Table 2.3: Class distribution of datasets

Datasets		Class					Total Attack	Total
		Normal	DoS	Probe	R2L	U2R		
Whole KDD	#Instance	972,780	3,883,370	41,102	1,126	52	3,925,650	4,898,430
	(%)	19.69	79.23	0.83	0.22	0.01	80.31	100
10% KDD	#Instance	97,278	391,458	4,107	1,126	52	396,743	494,021
	(%)	19.69	79.24	0.83	0.23	0.01	80.31	100
Uni KDD	#Instance	87,832	54,572	2,131	999	52	57,754	145,586
	(%)	60.33	37.48	1.46	0.69	0.035	39.67	100
Corrected Test	#Instance	60,593	229,853	4,166	16,347	70	250,436	311,029
	(%)	19.48	73.9	1.34	5.26	0.02	80.52	100
Uni Corr	#Instance	47,913	23,568	2,682	3,058	70	29,378	77,291
	(%)	61.99	30.49	3.47	3.96	0.09	38.01	100
NSL-KDD	Training	13449	9234	2289	209	11	11743	25192
	Testing	9711	7458	2421	2421	533	12833	22544

2.5.2 NSL-KDD dataset

NSL-KDD dataset (NSL-KDD, 2009) is refined version of KDD-Cup-1999 dataset, which is widely used for anomaly detection in NIDS. It contains selected and non-redundant records of KDD-Cup-1999 dataset with same number of features shown in Tables 2.3 and 2.4. Data preprocessing is an important step, which can be skipped by using this dataset. Hence, KDD-Cup-1999 dataset is selected for experiments to make a complete system, which consists of steps from preprocessing to final decision-making and more appropriate for real time.

2.6 PROPOSED HYBRID FEATURE SELECTION APPROACH (HyFSA)

2.6.1 HyFSA algorithm

A hybrid feature selection method, HyFSA is proposed, which utilizes fusion of four filter feature selection methods— CFS, CON, IG and GR (defined in Section

Table 2.4: Feature Number (#), Name and Type of features in KDD-Cup-1999

#	Name	Type	#	Name	Type	#	Name	Type
1	Duration	C	2	Protocol-type	D	3	Service	D
4	Flag	D	5	Src-bytes	C	6	Dst-bytes	C
7	Land	D	8	Wrong-fragment	C	9	Urgent	C
10	Hot	C	11	Num-failed-logins	C	12	Logged-in	D
13	Num-compromised	C	14	Root-shell	D	15	Su-attempted	D
16	Num-root	C	17	Num-file-creations	C	18	Num-shells	C
19	Num-access-files	C	20	Num-outbound-cmds	C	21	Is-hot-login	D
22	Is-guest-login	D	23	Count	C	24	Srv-count	C
25	Serror-rate	C	26	Srv-serror-rate	C	27	Rerror-rate	C
28	Srv-rerror-rate	C	29	Same-srv-rate	C	30	Diff-srv-rate	C
31	Srv-diff-host-rate	C	32	Dst-host-count	C	33	Dst-host-srv-count	C
34	Dst-host-same-srv-rate	C	35	Dst-host-diff-srv-rate	C	36	Dst-host-same-src-port-rate	C
37	Dst-host-srv-diff-host-rate	C	38	Dst-host-serror-rate	C	39	Dst-host-srv-serror-rate	C
40	Dst-host-rerror-rate	C	41	Dst-host-srv-rerror-rate	C			

Note : C : Continuous; D: Discrete.

2.2.1) and wrapper method employing classifier NB. The classifiers NB and C4.5 are used in this work (defined in Section 2.2.2).

First, the top ranked $N1$ features obtained by IG and top ranked $N2$ features obtained by GR based on their performance are selected. Then the common features from the feature sets of CFS, CON, $N1$ of IG, and $N2$ of GR are selected to create the initial feature set. Another set is created of left features, which are remained in the sets of CFS, CON, IG and GR. Further, wrapper based method using linear forward selection employing classifier NB is applied to find the final optimal feature set. The metrics used are TPR, FPR, TBM, and RMSE to select the final optimal feature set. The algorithm is presented as:

Algorithm 2.1 : Hybrid Feature Selection Approach (HyFSA)

Input: Dataset for feature selection

Output: A set of optimal features set that maximize TPR and minimizes FPR, TBM and ERR.

Method:

Step 1: Initialize $F_{full} = \{f_1, f_2, f_3, ..., f_N\}$ is the set of N features from original dataset.

Step 2: Apply CFS + BestFirst (defined in 2.2.1.1) on F_{full} to obtain feature subset. Let F_{CFS} be the set.

$$F_{CFS} = \{f_{cfs1}, f_{cfs2}, ..., f_{cfsn}\}, n << N$$

Step 3: Apply CON + BestFirst (defined in 2.2.1.2) on F_{full} to obtain feature subset. Let F_{CON} be the set.

$$F_{CON} = \{f_{con1}, f_{con2}, ..., f_{conm}\}, m << N$$

Step 4: Applying IG (defined in 2.2.1.3) on F_{full} to obtain feature's rank. Arranged the features in descending order of their rank and select top N1 features based on their performance. Let F_{IG} and $F_{IG(N1)}$ be the set.

$$F_{IG} = \{f_{IG1}, f_{IG2}, ..., f_{IGN}\}; F_{IG(N1)} = \{f_{IG1}, f_{IG2}, ..., f_{IGN1}\}$$

Step 5: Apply GR (defined in 2.2.1.4) on F_{full} to obtain feature's rank. Arranged the features in descending order of their rank and select top N2 features based on their performance. Let F_{GR} and $F_{GR(N2)}$ be the set.

$$F_{GR} = \{f_{GR1}, f_{GR2}, ..., f_{GRN}\}; F_{GR(N2)} = \{f_{GR1}, f_{GR2}, ..., f_{GRN2}\}$$

Step 6: Common features are obtained from the steps (2) and (3). Let $F_{CFS \cap CON}$ be the set of features. Similarly, common features are obtained from the steps (4) and (5). Let $F_{IG(N1) \cap GR(N2)}$ be the set.

$$F_{CFS \cap CON} = \left\{ F_{CFS} \cap F_{CON} \right\}; F_{IG(N1) \cap GR(N2)} = \left\{ F_{IG(N1)} \cap F_{GR(N2)} \right\}$$

Step 7: Take the common features from the two sets $F_{CFS \cap CON}$ and $F_{IG(N1) \cap GR(N2)}$ from step 6. This set is the initial set for wrapper method. Let F_{IniFea} be the set.

$$F_{IniFea} = \left\{ F_{CFS \cap CON} \cap F_{IG(N1) \cap GR(N2)} \right\}$$

Step 8: Let F_{Left} be the set of left p features that are remained from the four sets F_{CFS}, F_{CON}, $F_{IG(N1)}$ and $F_{GR(N2)}$ after selecting the common features at step 7.

$$F_{\cup} = \left\{ F_{CFS} \cup F_{CON} \cup F_{IG(N1)} \cup F_{GR(N2)} \right\};$$

$$F_{Left} = \left\{ F_{\cup} - F_{IniFea} \right\}; F_{Left} = \left\{ f_{Left1}, f_{Left2}, \ldots \ldots, f_{Leftp} \right\}$$

Step 9: Let $F_{Temp} = F_{IniFea} =;$ F_{Left} = set of left p features; Per_{Temp} = Performance of F_{Temp}; $F_{Current}$ = Empty set.

    for i=1 to p

    begin

        Select i^{th} feature from F_{Left} set.

        $F_{Current} = F_{Temp} \cup F_{Left\_i}$

        Compute performance of $F_{Current}$ as $Per_{Current}$ by classifier

        if $Per_{Current} > Per_{Temp}$ then

            $F_{Temp} = F_{Temp} \cup F_{Left\_i}$

        else

            $F_{Current} = F_{Temp}$

        end if

    end for

Step 10: The final optimal feature set is F_{Temp}. Let $F_{Final} = F_{Temp}$ be the final feature subset. Test the performance of F_{Final} by the classifier.

The experimental setup and experimental results and analysis for proposed HyFSA are described in Section 2.6.2 and 2.6.3 respectively.

2.6.2 Experimental setup

A machine learning tool, WEKA (Hall et al., 2009), is utilized to perform the steps of proposed HyFSA and for classifiers NB and C4.5. The following procedure is followed phasewise to implement the proposed method.

Phase 1: Preprocessing of dataset

Phase 2: Feature Selection using HyFSA

Phase 3: Feature Evaluation

2.6.2.1 Phase 1: Preprocessing of dataset

"10% KDD" dataset is selected for experiment and preprocessed to obtain optimal features to detect normal or attack network traffic i.e., binary-class (normal or attack) classification. It consists of 2 steps as follows:

1) Data transformation: Feature selection for attack or normal detection, the label of each attack connection records are transformed into label "attack".

2) Data reduction: "10% KDD" dataset contains redundant records. So, they are removed. The resultant dataset "Uni KDD" dataset is reduced to 145,586 from 494020 shown in Table 2.3.

2.6.2.2 Phase 2: Feature selection using HyFSA

Feature selection is performed as stated in the algorithm of proposed HyFSA (Section 2.6.1). The classifier NB is employed to assess the feature subsets obtained by HyFSA at different steps. The features obtained by IG and GR are ranked in descending order as depicted in Tables 2.5 and 2.6 respectively. The features {7, 9, 14, 15, 18, 20, 21, 22} from Tables 2.5 and 2.6 have 0 rank. Hence, only 33 features are appropriate for further processing. The TPR, FPR, and RMSE obtained by classifier NB of first N (where, N=1 to 33) number of features from Tables 2.5 and 2.6 are shown in Table 2.7. The numbers of features selected based on performance from Table 2.7 are 3 and 25 respectively shown in bold. Therefore 3 and 25 are values of N1 and N2 at steps 4 and 5 respectively. The selected feature subsets and performance of these subsets at each step by the HyFSA is depicted in Table 2.8. Finally, 6 features {3, 5, 6, 10, 13, 29} are selected by HyFSA.

Table 2.5: Feature number (#) and rank of features using IG+Ranker

S.No	#	Rank	S.No	#	Rank	S.No	#	Rank
1	5	0.777642	15	12	0.471499	29	13	0.007595
2	3	0.770687	16	36	0.311277	30	16	0.002307
3	29	0.76049	17	37	0.304817	31	19	0.001838
4	30	0.758437	18	32	0.301177	32	17	0.000493
5	23	0.724922	19	31	0.163721	33	11	0.000368
6	4	0.694624	20	24	0.108046	34	18	0
7	6	0.65357	21	41	0.069915	35	14	0
8	34	0.64756	22	1	0.038766	36	15	0
9	33	0.646073	23	40	0.036751	37	22	0
10	35	0.628309	24	27	0.0359	38	9	0
11	38	0.544408	25	28	0.034621	39	20	0
12	39	0.53976	26	2	0.033233	40	7	0
13	25	0.53894	27	10	0.010456	41	21	0
14	26	0.535155	28	8	0.010336			

Table 2.6: Feature number (#) and rank of features using GR+Ranker

S.No	#	Rank	S.No	#	Rank	S.No	#	Rank
1	30	0.6027	15	35	0.2372	29	19	0.0605
2	26	0.5641	16	37	0.2336	30	28	0.0604
3	25	0.5599	17	36	0.1703	31	40	0.0447
4	29	0.5146	18	32	0.1659	32	24	0.0308
5	4	0.5101	19	8	0.1587	33	17	0.0257
6	39	0.4781	20	31	0.1466	34	22	0
7	12	0.4716	21	13	0.1239	35	9	0
8	38	0.4536	22	10	0.096	36	7	0
9	3	0.317	23	41	0.0811	37	20	0
10	6	0.2763	24	1	0.0719	38	15	0

Continue ...

Table 2.6 – (*Continued*)

S.No	#	Rank	S.No	#	Rank	S.No	#	Rank
11	5	0.2701	25	27	0.0657	39	14	0
12	33	0.252	26	11	0.0647	40	18	0
13	23	0.251	27	2	0.062	41	21	0
14	34	0.2476	28	16	0.0611			

Table 2.7: Performance of first N1 and first N2 features by Classifier NB

SNo	#Feature	Performance of first N1 feature(s) from Table 2.5 (IG)			Performance of first N2 feature(s) from Table 2.6 (GR)		
		TPR (%)	FPR (%)	RMSE (%)	TPR (%)	FPR (%)	RMSE (%)
1	41	97.5	3.8	15.56	97.5	3.8	15.56
2	1	96.1	2.9	18.75	95.9	5.7	19.06
3	2	99.1	1.3	9.11	96.2	5.7	18.84
4	3	**99.1**	**1.2**	**9.40**	96.2	5.7	18.72
5	4	98.1	2.8	13.20	96.6	5.0	18.37
6	5	97.6	3.6	14.78	96.6	5.1	18.32
7	6	97.7	3.5	14.85	96.6	5.1	18.33
8	7	98.0	3.0	12.54	96.6	5.0	18.28
9	8	97.9	3.2	14.16	96.6	5.1	18.28
10	9	97.6	3.6	14.98	96.7	5.0	17.96
11	10	97.4	3.9	15.69	96.8	4.9	17.56
12	11	97.4	3.9	15.86	97.2	4.2	15.99
13	12	97.2	4.2	16.22	97.2	4.2	15.98
14	13	97.1	4.4	16.63	97.3	4.1	15.92
15	14	97.0	4.5	16.97	97.2	4.2	16.17
16	15	97.1	4.3	16.55	97.1	4.3	16.55
17	16	97.0	4.5	16.93	97.2	4.2	16.30
18	17	97.1	4.4	16.71	97.1	4.4	16.71
19	18	97.1	4.4	16.64	97.1	4.4	16.64
20	19	97.2	4.3	16.52	97.5	3.8	15.62
21	20	97.2	4.3	16.51	97.5	3.7	15.59
22	21	97.2	4.3	16.44	97.5	3.7	15.59
23	22	97.2	4.3	16.43	97.5	3.7	15.59

Continue ...

Table 2.7 – (*Continued*)

SNo	#Feature	Performance of first N1 feature(s) from Table 2.5 (IG)			Performance of first N2 feature(s) from Table 2.6 (GR)		
		TPR (%)	FPR (%)	RMSE (%)	TPR (%)	FPR (%)	RMSE (%)
24	23	97.2	4.2	16.43	97.6	3.7	15.52
25	24	97.2	4.2	16.43	97.6	3.7	15.52
26	25	97.2	4.3	16.46	**97.6**	**3.7**	**15.50**
27	26	97.1	4.3	16.65	97.6	3.7	15.50
28	27	97.1	4.3	16.66	97.5	3.8	15.58
29	28	97.5	3.8	15.57	97.5	3.8	15.58
30	29	97.5	3.8	15.56	97.5	3.8	15.60
31	30	97.5	3.8	15.56	97.5	3.8	15.60
32	31	97.5	3.8	15.56	97.5	3.8	15.61
33	32	97.5	3.8	15.56	97.5	3.8	15.56
34	33	97.5	3.8	15.56	97.5	3.8	15.56

Table 2.8: Performance and feature set selected by HyFSA

Steps	Feature Set	Methods	No. of Features	Obtained Features	TPR (%)	FPR (%)	RMSE (%)	TBM (sec)
1	All	-	41	-	97.5	3.8	15.56	1.44
2	F_{CFS}	CFS+ BestFirst	8	3, 4, 8, 12,13,26,29,30	97.4	3.8	15.72	0.12
3	F_{CON}	CON+ BestFirst	11	1,3,5,6,13,24,29,33,34, 35,38	98.3	2.6	12.75	0.16
4	$F_{IG(33)}$	IG+Ranker	33	5,3,29,30,23,4,6,34,33, 35,38,39,25,26,12,36,37, 32,31,24,41,1,40,27,28, 2,10,8,13, 16,19,17,11	97.5	3.8	15.56	0.34
4	$F_{IG(3)}$	IG+Ranker	3	5,3,29	99.1	1.2	9.4	0.08
5	$F_{GR(33)}$	GR+Ranker	33	30,26,25,29,4,39,12,38, 3,6,5,33,23,34,35,37,36, 32,8,31,13,10,41,1,27, 11,2,16, 19, 28,40,24,17	97.5	3.8	15.56	0.36

Continue ...

Table 2.8 – (Continued)

Steps	Feature Set	Methods	No. of Features	Obtained Features	TPR (%)	FPR (%)	RMSE (%)	TBM (sec)
5	$F_{GR(25)}$	GR+Ranker	25	30,26,25,29,4,39,12,38, 3,6,5,33,23,34,35,37,36, 32,8,31,13,10,41,1,27	97.6	3.7	15.5	0.25
6	$F_{CFS \cap CON}$	-	3	3,13,29	96.4	4.6	16.21	0.08
6	$F_{IG(3)}$ $\cap GR(25)$	-	3	3,5,29	99.1	1.2	9.4	0.08
7	F_{IniFea}	-	4	3,5,13,29	99.2	1.2	9.05	0.09
8	$F_{\cup}$	-	26	1,3,4,5,6,8,10,12,13,23, 24,25,26,27,29,30,31,32, 33,34,35,36,37,38,39,41	97.5	3.7	15.47	0.27
8	F_{Left}	-	22	1,4,6,8,10,12,23,24,25, 26,27,30,31,32, 33,34, 35,36,37,38,39,41	97.1	4.4	16.78	0.22
9	F_{Temp}	Wrapper + LFS+NB	6	3,5,6,10,13,29	99.4	0.8	6.98	0.10
10	F_{Final}	**HyFSA**	**6**	**3,5,6,10,13,29**	**99.4**	**0.8**	**6.98**	**0.10**

2.6.2.3 Phase 3: Feature evaluation

The NB and C4.5 classifiers are employed to evaluate the optimal feature subset in terms of TPR, FPR, TBM, ACC, ERR, and RMSE using 10-fold cross validation.

2.6.3 Experimental results and analysis

The HyFSA, CFS, CON, IG, and GR are applied on 41 features of "Uni KDD" dataset. The obtained features are 6, 8, 11, 3, and 25 by HyFSA, CFS, CON, IG, and GR respectively. The performance in terms of TPR, FPR, TBM and RMSE of obtained feature subsets at each step of HyFSA are shown in Table 2.8. The final six features {3, 5, 6, 10, 13, and 29} are obtained by HyFSA, which is 15% of the original feature set. The performance of 6 features assessed by classifiers NB and C4.5 are depicted in Tables 2.9 and 2.10 respectively. The HyFSA is also compared with CFS, CON, IG and GR on reduced feature set. There is increase in TPR and decrease in FPR, ERR, and RMSE of the classifiers on features set obtained by HyFSA than full set, CFS, CON, IG, and GR (Tables 2.9 and 2.10). The TBM is also reduced to 88% approximately. The Figures 2.7 to 2.12 show comparative graph for classifiers NB and C4.5 in terms of TPR, ACC, FPR, ERR, TBM, and RMSE on feature subsets selected by CFS, CON, IG, GR, full set, and HyFSA respectively. Results demonstrate that selected 6 features from HyFSA outperforms CSF, CON, IG, GR and full set.

Table 2.9: Performance of NB on different feature sets

Metrics	Feature Selection Method (# Feature)					
	Full Set (41)	CFS (8)	CON (11)	IG (3)	GR (25)	HyFSA (6)
TPR (%)	97.5	97.4	98.3	99.1	97.6	**99.4**
FPR (%)	3.8	3.8	2.6	1.2	3.7	**0.8**
TBM(sec)	1.44	0.12	0.16	0.08	0.25	0.10
ACC (%)	97.51	97.44	98.26	99.15	97.57	**99.44**
ERR (%)	2.49	2.56	1.74	0.85	2.43	**0.56**
RMSE(%)	15.56	15.72	12.75	9.40	15.50	**6.98**

Table 2.10: Performance of C4.5 on different feature sets

Metrics	Feature Selection Method (# Feature)					
	Full Set (41)	CFS (8)	CON (11)	IG (3)	GR (25)	HyFSA (6)
TPR (%)	99.8	98.9	99.8	99.8	99.8	**99.9**
FPR (%)	0.2	1.4	0.2	0.2	0.2	**0.2**
TBM (sec)	8.71	1.19	1.37	1.08	3.46	**0.63**
ACC (%)	99.84	98.88	99.83	99.85	99.82	99.86
ERR (%)	0.16	1.12	0.17	0.15	0.18	**0.14**
RMSE (%)	3.82	9.34	3.97	3.52	4.03	**3.48**

2.7 PROPOSED HETEROGENEOUS ENSEMBLE OF INTELLIGENT CLASSIFIERS (HEIC)

2.7.1 HEIC algorithm

The HEIC is proposed to enhance the performance of classifier in terms of increased ACC and decreased FPR and FNR of NIDS to detect intrusion from network

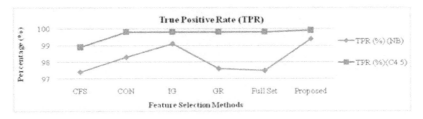

Figure 2.7: Comparison of TPR

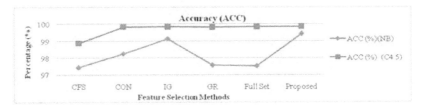

Figure 2.8: Comparison of ACC

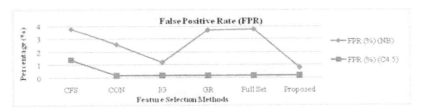

Figure 2.9: Comparison of FPR

Figure 2.10: Comparison of ERR

traffic. A novel heterogeneous ensemble is presented, which combines the decisions of multiple diverse and accurate classifiers in HEIC. A parallel ensemble structure is employed to construct it. It contains following two steps:

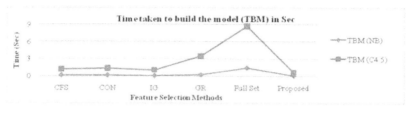

Figure 2.11: Comparison of TBM (in sec.)

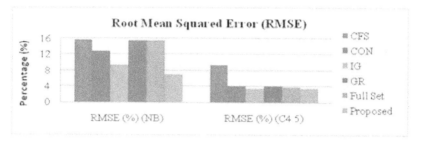

Figure 2.12: Comparison of RMSE

1 : Selection of base classifiers for ensemble

2 : Ensemble and combiner method

1) Selection of base classifiers for ensemble

Different classifiers are compared to select accurate and diverse base classifiers. Motivation of selecting different base classifiers leads diversity in constructing heterogeneous ensemble. Each classifier selected in this step has different learning hypotheses and inductive bias, which make diverse set of classifiers for ensemble.

2) Step 2: Ensemble and combiner method

In this, decisions of individual classifiers are combined to classify input instance. The decision of diverse classifiers are combined by elementary combiners empolying algebraic combination rules to produce accurate and reliable final decision. A parallel ensemble structure is employed to construct the heterogeneous ensemble. In this, every classifier is trained independently on training dataset. Then elementary combiners are used to combine the decisions of these classifiers to yield the final decision. Elementary Combiners—Average, Product, Minimum, Maximum, and Majority Voting are employed as combiner to yield final decision.

2.7.2 Experimental setup

Weka is used as tool for classifiers and ensembles utilized in this method. "10% KDD" dataset is selected for experiment. The following procedure is followed phasewise to implement the proposed method.

Phase 1: Preprocessing of dataset

Phase 2: Model development using HEIC

Phase 3: Evaluation of classifiers and ensembles

2.7.2.1 Phase 1: Preprocessing of dataset

The "10% KDD" dataset is preprocessed for classification of normal or attack detection. It consists of 3 steps.

1) Data transformation: The label of each attack connection records are transformed into label "attack".

2) Data reduction: The resultant dataset contains around 70% redundant records. Therefore, these records are removed from the dataset. The resultant datasets named as "Uni KDD" is shown in Table 2.3.

3) Creation of training and test dataset: "Uni KDD" is equally divided into two datasets: the training dataset ("Uni Train") and test dataset ("Uni Test") for 41 features, each containing 72793 records.

2.7.2.2 Phase 2: Model development using HEIC

This phase consists of two steps.

1) Selection of base classifiers for ensemble

The C4.5 based on DT, NB based on probability theory, NN-SGD based on soft computing, k-NN instance based, RIPPER based on rules and RF based on homogeneous ensemble of decision trees briefly discussed in Section 2.4.2 are selected as base classifiers for the ensemble. These classifiers have different learning hypotheses and inductive bias.

The performance of k-NN classifier is influenced by the value of the parameter k, the number of most similar neighbours of the new input pattern. In order to select the value of k, the experimental results of k-NN for different k values varied from 1 to 25 for odd number using 5-fold cross validation on "Uni Train" dataset are compared. The selected value of k for k-NN is 3 based minimum errors and maximum ACC (Table 2.11) except $k = 1$ as it badly overfits the classifier. The ACC, RMSE, and FPR of k-NN for different values of k is shown in Figure 2.13. Euclidean distance is used to find the nearest neighbours. Euclidean distance $d(a, b)$ between two instances a and b is defined as

$$d(a, b) = \sqrt{\sum_{i=1}^{N} \delta_i{}^2} \qquad (2.28)$$

where δ_i is the difference of ith feature's value of a and b and N is number of features in the dataset. The δ_i can be calculated for numerical and nominal feature as

$$\delta_i = \begin{cases} x_i - y_i, & \text{for numerical feature} \\ 0, & \text{if } x_i = y_i \text{ for nominal feature} \\ 1, & \text{if } x_i \neq y_i \text{ for nominal feature} \end{cases} \qquad (2.29)$$

These classifiers are trained on "Uni Train" dataset. The TPR, FPR, ACC, PRE, ROC, TBM, TTM and RMSE are used to compare the results of classifiers on training dataset "Uni Train" as depicted in Table 2.12.

2) Ensemble and combiner method

The Average, Product, Majority Voting, Minimum, and Maximum are employed to combine the decisions of 5 classifiers—NB, NN-SGD, RIPPER, C4.5 and RF out of 6 classifiers to construct the ensemble (detail in Section 2.7.3). The results of these ensembles on "Uni Train" dataset in terms of TPR, FPR, ACC, PRE, ROC, TBM, TTM and RMSE are illustrated in Table 2.13.

Table 2.11: Performance of k-NN classifier for different values of k

k-NN	Evaluation Metrics					
Classifier	TPR (%)	FPR (%)	ACC (%)	PRE (%)	ROC (%)	RMSE (%)
k=1	99.8	0.2	99.8	99.85	99.8	4.52
k=3	99.7	0.3	99.74	99.7	99.9	4.44
k=5	99.7	0.3	99.72	99.7	99.9	4.55
k=7	99.7	0.3	99.72	99.7	99.9	4.65
k=9	99.7	0.4	99.7	99.7	99.9	4.8
k=11	99.7	0.4	99.67	99.7	99.9	4.97
k=13	99.7	0.4	99.67	99.7	99.9	4.97
k=15	99.6	0.5	99.64	99.6	100	5.26
k=17	99.6	0.5	99.61	99.6	100	5.4
k=19	99.6	0.5	99.6	99.6	100	5.5
k=21	99.6	0.5	99.59	99.6	100	5.61
k=23	99.6	0.5	99.58	99.6	99.9	5.73
k=25	99.6	0.6	99.57	99.6	100	5.84

Table 2.12: Performance of classifiers on training dataset using 41 features

Metrics	Classifiers					
	NB	NN-SGD	k-NN(k=3)	RIPPER	C4.5	RF
TPR (%)	97.0	99.5	99.9	99.9	99.9	99.9
FPR (%)	3.8	0.5	0.1	0.2	0.1	0.1
ACC (%)	96.99	99.47	99.87	99.85	99.91	99.93
PRE (%)	97.0	99.5	99.9	99.9	99.9	99.9
ROC (%)	97.6	99.5	100.0	99.9	100.0	100.0
TBM (sec)	2.56	541.43	**0.08**	171.51	40.34	952.99
TTM (sec)	6.74	29.87	**15781.1**	0.64	0.58	146.05
RMSE (%)	17.28	7.25	2.84	3.78	2.9	2.56

2.7.2.3 Phase 3: Evaluation of the classifiers and ensembles

The test dataset "Uni Test" is employed to evaluate the effectiveness of classifiers and ensembles. The TPR, FPR, ACC, PRE, ROC and RMSE are used to assess the performance of these classifiers and constructed ensembles on test dataset "Uni Test" for 41 features as shown in Tables 2.14 and 2.15 respectively.

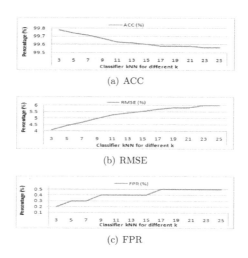

(a) ACC

(b) RMSE

(c) FPR

Figure 2.13: (a) ACC, (b) RMSE and (c) FPR of k-NN

Table 2.13: Performance of ensembles on training dataset using 41 features

Metrics	Ensemble of Classifiers				
	Average	Product	Majority Voting	Minimum	Maximum
TPR (%)	100.0	99.8	100.0	99.8	98.1
FPR (%)	0.0	0.2	0.0	0.2	2.8
ACC (%)	99.97	99.47	99.97	99.47	98.15
PRE (%)	100.0	99.8	100.0	99.8	98.2
ROC (%)	100.0	99.7	100.0	99.7	100.0
TBM (s)	626.23	590.15	541.61	616.26	599.57
TTM (s)	21.5	17.86	20.34	21.08	18.08
RMSE(%)	4.29	3.91	1.85	3.91	9.17

2.7.3 Experimental results and analysis

Several experiments have been performed to assess the performance of HEIC proposed in Section 2.7.1 in terms of efficiency and accuracy. All experiments are conducted using Weka. The "Uni Train" and "Uni Test" datasets are used in the experiments for training and testing respectively.

Table 2.14: Performance of classifiers on test dataset using 41 features

Metrics	Classifiers					
	NB	NN-SGD	k-NN (k=3)	RIPPER	C4.5	RF
TPR (%)	97.1	99.5	99.8	99.9	99.9	100.0
FPR (%)	3.7	0.5	0.2	0.1	0.1	0.1
ACC (%)	97.06	99.48	99.81	99.92	99.87	99.96
PRE (%)	97.1	99.5	99.8	99.9	99.9	100.0
ROC (%)	97.6	99.5	99.9	99.9	99.9	100.0
RMSE(%)	17.07	7.24	3.94	2.81	3.33	2.15

Table 2.15: Performance of ensembles on test dataset using 41 features

Metrics	Ensemble of Classifiers				
	Average	Product	Majority Voting	Minimum	Maximum
TPR (%)	99.9	99.8	99.9	99.8	98.1
FPR (%)	0.1	0.2	0.1	0.2	2.8
ACC (%)	99.94	99.45	99.94	99.45	98.15
PRE (%)	99.9	99.8	99.9	99.8	98.2
ROC (%)	100.0	99.6	99.9	99.6	100.0
RMSE(%)	4.44	4.44	2.49	4.44	9.19

The training and testing are carried out for 6 classifiers and 5 ensembles using 41 features and then compared on different evaluation metrics. Tables 2.12 and 2.14 illustrate the performances of these six classifiers trained on "Uni Train" dataset and tested on "Uni Test" test dataset using different evaluation metrics respectively. It is evident that classifier RF (TPR=99.9%, ACC=99.93%, PRE=99.9%, FPR=0.1%, ROC=100.0%, RMSE of 2.56%) is better than other five classifiers on all performance metrics except TBM and TTM. The k-NN has minimum TBM of 0.08 sec. Apart from this, C4.5 has minimum TTM of 0.58 sec and NB has minimum TBM of 2.56 sec among all classifiers (Table 2.12). The classifiers C4.5, RF, and k-NN achieved ROC of 100.0%, C4.5 yielded PRE (99.9%) and TPR (99.9%). Comparative graph of classifiers for TPR, ACC, PRE, and ROC for 41 features are shown in Figure 2.14, RMSE and FPR in Figure 2.15. The performances of classifiers NB and NN-SGD are little bit higher in testing phase (Table 2.14) than training phase (Table 2.12), whereas classifiers k-NN, RIPPER, C4.5, and RF performed near to equal in training as well as in testing phase.

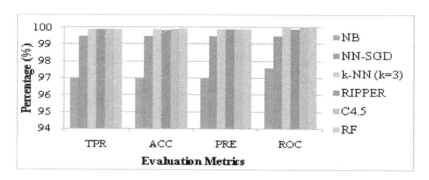

Figure 2.14: TPR, ACC, PRE and ROC of classifiers

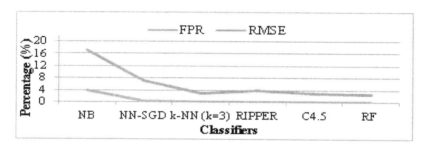

Figure 2.15: FPR and RMSE of classifiers

The k-NN has highest TTM (5087.73 sec.) among six classifiers, which is extraordinarily very high. It will increase the computation time and reduce the performance of HEIC. Hence, it is not appropriate as base classifier in ensemble for real-time processing for large volume network traffic. As a result, 5 base classifiers—NB, NN-SGD, RIPPER, C4.5 and RF are selected to build HEIC. Finally, five ensemble models are constructed by using 5 combiners (Average, Product, Majority Voting, Minimum, and Maximum), each employing selected five classifiers. Table 2.13 illustrates the results of these 5 ensemble models using all 41 features on training dataset "Uni Train" based on different evaluation metrics.

The ensembles using Majority Voting and Average yielded equally best performance for ACC (99.97%), PRE (100.0%), TPR (100.0%), FPR (0.0%), and ROC

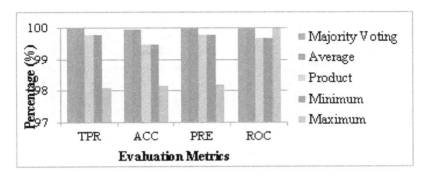

Figure 2.16: TPR, ACC, PRE and ROC of ensembles

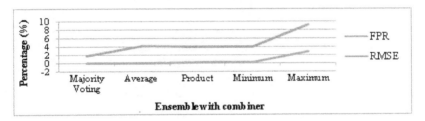

Figure 2.17: FPR and RMSE of ensembles

(100.0%) on 41 features among all 5 ensemble models. Majority voting combiner has the lowest RMSE of 1.85% for 41 features (Table 2.13). Maximum combiner has yielded the lowest performance on all evaluation metrics except ROC (100.0%). Whereas, Minimum and Product combiners' performance degraded because of 275 (0.38%) unclassified instances. Therefore, the best performing ensemble model is using Majority Voting on overall performance. The TPR, ACC, PRE, and ROC of ensembles is shown in Figure 2.16 and for FPR and RMSE in Figure 2.17. The performances of ensembles evaluated using test dataset "Uni Test" for 41 features on different performance evaluation measures are shown in Table 2.15. The performances of the ensembles in testing phase (Table 2.15) are almost the same to training phase (Table 2.13).

On the comparison of results of 5 ensemble models (Tables 2.13 & 2.15) and 6 classifiers (Tables 2.12 & 2.14) based on different evaluation metrics show that ensemble using Majority Voting outperformed individual classifiers and other ensemble models. Hence, it is more reliable and capable for NIDS and therefore selected as ensemble model to construct HEIC. The TPR, ACC, PRE, & ROC of classifiers NB, NN-SGD, RIPPER, C4.5, RF and proposed HEIC is shown in Figure 2.18 and FPR and RMSE in Figure 2.19. The emperical results strongly indicate that by employing HEIC to build the model has been enhanced the performance with TRP (100.0%), ACC (99.97%), PRE (100.0%), ROC (100.0%), with extremely low FPR (0.0%) and RMSE (1.85%).

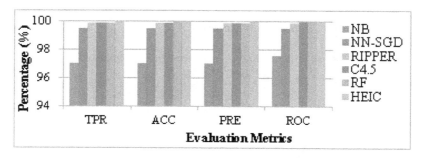

Figure 2.18: TPR, ACC, PRE & ROC of classifiers & HEIC

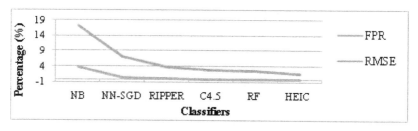

Figure 2.19: FPR & RMSE of of classifiers & HEIC

2.8 PROPOSED HYBRID SAMPLING CLASS BALANCER ALGORITHM (HySCBA)

2.8.1 HySCBA algorithm

An algorithm based on hybrid sampling technique for multi-class imbalanced dataset, HySCBA, is proposed. It integrates random under-sampling for the majority class and over-sampling for minority class to balance the class distribution of multi-class imbalanced dataset. The proposed HySCBA is presented in Algorithm 2.2.

The HySCBA algorithm proceeds as follows. There are two inputs—Dataset D with n number of classes and number of instances as $Balance_{Instance}$ to balance the class distribution. Subsequently, find the rarest class from the dataset. Let it be C_r. For all majority classes (number of instances more than $Balance_{Instance}$), Spread Subsample under-sampling technique is applied to balance the number of instances equal to the $Balance_{Instance}$. Spread Subsample technique requires "distribution spread", $Distribution_{Spread}$ parameter. It randomly selects the instances equal to product of $Distribution_{Spread}$ and instances in C_r for each class having instances more than $Balance_{Instance}$. For all minority classes (number of instances less than $Balance_{Instance}$), SMOTE over-sampling technique is applied for each minority class to balance the number of instances equal to the $Balance_{Instance}$. SMOTE requires "percentage" parameter to create synthetic instances of each minority class such that it becomes equal to $Balance_{Instance}$. For the classes having number of instances equal to $Balance_{Instance}$ are left unprocessed.

Algorithm 2.2 : Hybrid Sampling Class Balancer Algorithm (HySCBA) for multi-class imbalanced dataset

---

Input: Multi-class dataset D with n number of classes; Number of instances to balance the class distribution, $Balance_{Instance}$.

Output: Balanced Dataset BD with n number of classes, having approximately $Balance_{Instance}$ for each class.

Method:

Step 1: Input the multi-class dataset D with n number of classes and number of instances to balance the class distribution of all classes equal to it. Let it be $Balance_{Instance}$. Let the classes are $C_1, C_2, C_3, ..., C_n$.

Step 2: Find the rarest class (class with minimum number of instances). Let it be C_r.

Under-sampling : for all majority class(es)

Step 3: Calculate distribution spread, $Distribution_{Spread}$, according to following formula:

$$Distribution_{Spread} = \frac{Balance_{Instance}}{\#\text{Instances of } C_r}$$

Step 4: Apply random under-sampling method using Spread Subsample by setting parameter "distribution spread" equal to $Distribution_{Spread}$ and taking other parameter as default. It produces temporary dataset D_t in which number of instances become equal to $Balance_{Instance}$ for all class $C_i, i = 1, 2, ..., n$ where number of instances of $C_i > Balance_{Instance}$.

Over-sampling : for all minority class(es)

Step 5: For each $C_i, i = 1, 2, ..., n$ where number of instances of $C_i < Balance_{Instance}$, perform following steps:

Step 5.1: Select the rarest class, let it be C_m as minority class, from the updated dataset D_t.

Step 5.2: Compute the percentage of instances, $Per_{Minority}$, to create number of new samples for minority class to balance the class distribution, according to following formula:

$$Per_{Minority} == \left(\frac{Balance_{Instance}}{\#\text{ Instances of } C_m} - 1\right) * 100$$

Step 5.3: Apply SMOTE by setting parameter "percentage" equal to $Per_{Minority}$ and taking other parameter as default.

Step 5.4: Update the dataset, let it be D_t.

Step 6: Final balance dataset, BD = Dt. Return BD.

The experimental setup and experimental results and analysis for proposed HySCBA are in described Sections 2.8.2 and 2.8.3 respectively.

2.8.2 Experimental setup

WEKA is used to compute the Spread Subsample under-sampling technique and SMOTE over-sampling technique and for classifiers NB and C4.5 to assess the classification performance on datasets obtained at various steps of proposed HySCBA. The following procedure is followed as:

Phase 1: Preprocessing of dataset

Phase 2: Balance class distribution using HySCBA

Phase 3: Evaluation of HySCBA

2.8.2.1 Phase 1: Preprocessing of dataset

The "10% KDD" dataset selected for experiments is described in Section 2.5. It is preprocessed for attack class classification (detection of specific attack type). This phase contains 2 steps.

1) Data transformation: For attack class classification, the label of each attack connection for all types of attack are transformed into specific attack types (DoS, Probe, R2l, U2R) according to Table 2.2.

2) Data reduction: For attack class classification, dataset must contain only attack types, so normal connection records are removed from dataset. The resultant dataset is named as "Atk KDD" shown in Table 2.16. This "Atk KDD" dataset also consists of around 85% redundant connection records shown in Table 2.3. Since connection records of Probe, R2L and U2R are very less in numbers with comparison to DoS attack, therefore redundant connection records of only DoS attack are removed. The resultant datasets named as "Atk Uni KDD" shown in Table 2.16.

2.8.2.2 Phase 2: Balance class distribution using HySCBA

The "Atk Uni KDD" dataset contains four classes (DoS, Probe, R2L and U2R), with 54572, 4107, 1126 and 52 instances respectively. This dataset has a high level of imbalance and contains one majority and three minority classes. The balance of class distribution is done according to the proposed HySCBA (Section 2.8.1). The classifiers NB and C4.5 are used to evaluate the different datasets obtained at different steps of proposed HySCBA.

Step 1: The "Atk Uni KDD" dataset contains four classes as C_1, C_2, C_3 and C_4. The value of $Balance_{Instance}$ is 5000.

Step 2: The rarest class (class with minimum number of samples) is U2R i.e., C_4.

Step 3: The calculated value of $Distribution_{Spread}$ is 96.15.

Step 4: Only one class C_1 (DoS) is majority class, has number of instance more than $Balance_{Instance}$. Therefore random under-sampling method using Spread Subsample by setting parameter "distribution spread" equal to 96.15 and taking other parameter as default is applied. It produces temporary dataset D_t as shown in Table 2.16 (Dataset D_t at Step 4).

Step 5: There are 3 minority classes as Probe (C_2), R2L (C_3) and U2R (C_4) have number of instance less than $Balance_{Instance}$. For each $C_i, i = 2, 3, 4$, following steps are performed :

For C_4

Step 5.1: The rarest class among C_2, C_3 and C_4 is C_4.

Step 5.2: The calculated $Per_{Minority}$ is 9515.

Step 5.3: The SMOTE is applied by setting parameter "percentage" equal 9515 and taking other parameter as default.

Step 5.4: It produces temporary dataset D_t as shown in Table 2.16 (Dataset D_t at Step 5 for C_4).

For C_3

Step 5.1: The rarest class is C_3.

Step 5.2: The calculated $Per_{Minority}$ is 344.

Step 5.3: The SMOTE is applied by setting parameter "percentage" equal 344 and taking other parameter as default.

Step 5.4: It produces temporary dataset D_t as shown in Table 2.16 (Dataset D_t at Step 5 for C_3).

For C_2

Step 5.1: The rarest class is C_2.

Step 5.2: The calculated $Per_{Minority}$ is 21.

Step 5.3: The SMOTE is applied by setting parameter "percentage" equal 21 and taking other parameter as default.

Step 5.4: It produces temporary dataset D_t as shown in Table 2.16 (Dataset D_t at Step 5 for C_2).

Step 6: The resultant balanced dataset, BD, by HySCBA in Table 2.16 at step 6.

Table 2.16: Statistics of each attack type at different steps of HySCBA

Attack Name	Dataset						
	Atk KDD	Atk Uni KDD	Dataset Dt at Step 4	Dataset Dt at Step 5 for C4	Dataset Dt at Step 5 for C3	Dataset Dt at Step 5 for C2	Final Dataset DB by HySCBA at Step 6
DoS	391,458	54,572	4,999	4,999	4,999	4,999	4,999
Probe	4,107	4,107	4,107	4,107	4,107	5,010	5,010
R2L	1,126	1,126	1,126	1,126	4,999	4,999	4,999
U2R	52	52	52	4,999	4,999	4,999	4,999
Total	396,743	59, 857	10,284	15,231	19,104	20,007	20,007

2.8.2.3 Phase 3: Evaluation of HySCBA

The classifiers NB and C4.5 are used for evaluation. The performance of HySCBA is assesses in terms of GM, PRE, F1-S and PRC (defined in Section 2.4) by classifiers NB and C4.5 using 10-fold cross validation.

2.8.3 Experimental results and analysis

The class distribution of the datasets obtained at different steps by proposed HySCBA is shown in Table 2.16. The final dataset contains approximately equal class distribution of four classes of attacks. The performances of classifiers NB and C4.5 without employing any sampling algorithm and HySCBA evaluated in terms of GM, PRE, F1-S and PRC using 10-fold cross validation on "Atk Uni KDD" is shown in Table 2.17. Result shows that C4.5 outperforms NB in all evaluation metrics. It can be seen from Table 2.17 that classifiers perform better when employed with proposed HySCBA than without using any sampling algorithm except DoS attack. The reason is as it has significantly out numbers the number of instances of other classes (Probe, R2L and U2R) when no sampling algorithm is applied.

Table 2.17: Performance of classifiers NB and C4.5

	Classifiers ->	NB		C4.5	
	Algorithm ->	No	Proposed	No	Proposed
Evaluation Metrics	Attack Name	Sampling	HySCBA	Sampling	HySCBA
GM(%)	U2R	94.1	88.4	90.9	**99.8**
	DoS	97.9	97.6	99.7	**99.8**
	R2L	60.3	**64.8**	99.1	**99.7**
	Probe	94.7	**98.6**	99.8	**99.8**
PRE(%)	U2R	3.7	**63.0**	79.6	**99.6**
	DoS	100.0	99.3	100.0	99.8
	R2L	42.9	**96.1**	99.4	**99.8**
	Probe	73.8	**93.3**	99.6	**99.7**
F1-S(%)	U2R	7.1	**76.2**	81.1	**99.7**
	DoS	98.1	97.4	100.0	99.8
	R2L	39.5	**58.8**	98.8	99.7
	Probe	81.8	**96.4**	99.6	**99.7**
PRC(%)	U2R	22.3	**92.3**	68.0	**99.4**
	DoS	100.0	98.3	100.0	99.9
	R2L	57.9	**89.2**	98.7	99.7
	Probe	78.1	**99.7**	99.6	99.6

The proposed HySCBA is compared with *SpreadSubsample* random under-sampling and SMOTE algorithm. The proposed HySCBA is also compared with the case in which no sampling technique is used to deal with class imbalanced problem using "Atk KDD" and "Atk Uni KDD" datasets. We have used the value of parameter spread as 100 and the value of other parameters is set to default value in *SpreadSubsample* random under-sampling method. The value of the parameters for SMOTE method is set to default value. The "Atk KDD" dataset is employed in *SpreadSubsample* and SMOTE methods. Tables 2.18 and 2.19 show the performance of classifiers NB and C4.5 in terms of GM, PRE, F1-S and PRC obtained by using—no sampling technique, *SpreadSubsample*, SMOTE and proposed HySCBA using 10-fold cross validation. Result shows that C4.5 outperforms NB in all evaluation metrics as shown in Tables 2.18 and 2.19. Tables 2.18 and 2.19 indicate that the proposed HySCBA consistently produced best results in term of used evaluation metrics when applied to "Atk KDD" dataset except DoS. The reason is as DoS has lesser number of instances in proposed HySCBA than the number of instances in other algorithms. Furthermore, the classifiers consistently perform poor on original highly imbalanced datasets in which no sampling algorithm is employed specially for minority classes. The performance of classifiers also increases in terms of all evaluation metrics for minority classes by employing Spread Subsample under-sampling algorithm as can be seen in Tables 2.18 and 2.19. But SMOTE does not perform well.

Table 2.18: Experimental results of classifier NB for different algorithm

Metrics	Attack Name	Algorithm				
		No Sampling (Atk KDD)	No Sampling (Atk Uni KDD)	Spread Subsample	SMOTE	Proposed HySCBA
GM(%)	U2R	93.9	94.1	88.8	97.4	88.4
	DoS	96.7	97.9	96.9	96.4	97.6
	R2L	60.0	60.3	61.5	61.7	**64.8**
	Probe	92.8	94.7	92.8	93.6	**98.6**
PRE(%)	U2R	3.6	3.7	4.6	8.4	**63.0**
	DoS	100.0	100.0	99.3	100.0	99.3
	R2L	37.1	42.9	92.4	17.4	**96.1**
	Probe	14.6	73.8	91.3	15.0	**93.3**
F1-S(%)	U2R	6.9	7.1	8.8	15.5	**76.2**
	DoS	97.0	98.1	96.8	96.9	97.4
	R2L	36.6	39.5	53.9	24.0	**58.8**
	Probe	25.2	81.8	91.3	25.8	**96.4**
PRC(%)	U2R	20.2	22.3	26.1	64.0	**92.3**
	DoS	100.0	100.0	99.6	100.0	98.3
	R2L	42.0	57.9	92.7	22.3	89.2
	Probe	71.4	78.1	98.0	73.6	97.7

Table 2.19: Experimental results of classifier C4.5 for different algorithm

Metrics	Attack Name	Algorithm				
		No Sampling (Atk KDD)	No Sampling (Atk Uni KDD)	Spread Subsample	SMOTE	Proposed HySCBA
GM(%)	U2R	89.9	90.9	85.5	93.5	**99.8**
	DoS	99.6	99.7	99.8	99.6	**99.8**
	R2L	99.3	99.1	99.3	99.1	**99.7**
	Probe	99.6	99.8	99.8	99.6	**99.8**
PRE(%)	U2R	87.5	79.6	79.2	89.2	**99.6**
	DoS	100.0	100.0	99.9	100.0	99.8
	R2L	98.9	99.4	98.5	99.1	**99.8**
	Probe	99.8	99.6	99.7	99.8	99.7
F1-S(%)	U2R	84.1	81.1	76.0	88.3	**99.7**
	DoS	100.0	100.0	99.8	100.0	99.8
	R2L	98.8	98.8	98.6	98.7	99.7
	Probe	99.6	99.6	99.8	99.6	99.7
PRC(%)	U2R	74.2	68.0	68.4	87.0	**99.4**
	DoS	100.0	100.0	99.9	100.0	99.9
	R2L	98.4	98.7	98.5	99.2	**99.7**
	Probe	99.7	99.6	99.6	99.6	99.6

The comparative graphs for the performance of classifiers NB and C4.5 in terms of GM and PRE are shown in Figures 2.20 and 2.22, for F1-S and PRC in Figures 2.21 and 2.23 respectively by employing sampling algorithm as (i) No sampling algorithm using "Atk KDD" dataset (ii) No sampling algorithm using "Atk Uni KDD" dataset (iii) Spread Subsample (iv) SMOTE and (v) Proposed HySCBA. Results show that proposed HySCBA outperforms no sampling algorithm, Spread Subsample and SMOTE for attack classes except DoS.

2.9 SUMMARY

This chapter discussed in detail the foundations of the methods / topics used in this research. It included introduction of feature selection and discussed relevant methods like CFS, CON, IG and GR. It also described classifiers like NB, DT,

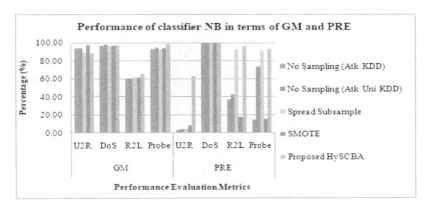

Figure 2.20: GM and PRE of NB for different algorithms

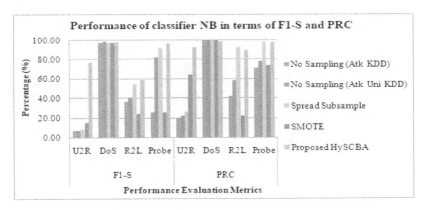

Figure 2.21: F1-S and PRC of NB for different algorithms

RF, ANN, k-NN, and RIPPER. The chapter also described ensemble of classifiers and methods for combating class imbalanced problem in multi-class case. After this, the system architecture design of research work for anomaly based NIDPS is presented. For this research work, the system architecture is modeled and designed with the three major modules— (i) Module I: Methodology for NIDS to detect normal or attack traffic, (ii) Module II: Methodology for NIDS to detect specific attack type, and (iii) Module III: Methodology for IPS to prevent from identified attack traffic. Then, the chapter described the evaluation metrics used to evaluate the proposed work and datasets (KDD-Cup-1999 and NSL-KDD) used

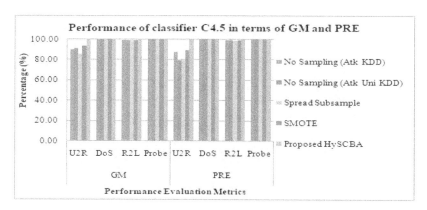

Figure 2.22: GM and PRE of C4.5 for different algorithms

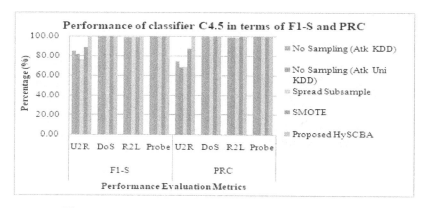

Figure 2.23: F1-S and PRC of C4.5 for different algorithms

in the experiments. Further, the chapter discussed proposed HyFSA, HEIC, and HySCBA.

The proposed HyFSA selected only 6 significant features from the original 41 features. The result achieved by 6 features obtained by HyFSA outperformed CFS, CON, IG and GR. The TPR (%) are 99.4 and 99.9 and for FPRs (%) are 0.8 and 0.2 by classifiers NB and C4.5 respectively. Only 6 features are sufficient to detect normal or attack from network traffic. The HEIC utilized classifiers NB, NN-SGD, RIPPER, C4.5 and RF and their decisions are fused by Majority Voting. The results demonstrated that HEIC outperformed single classifiers and other ensemble methods. It improved the TPR (100.0%), PRE(100.0%), ACC (99.97%), and ROC(100.0%) and reduced the RMSE (1.85%) and FPR (0.0%). The proposed HySA-CBMCD improved the performance of classifiers on multi-class imbalanced dataset specially for rare classes. Therefore sampling method is required to balance the class distribution of the dataset in order to improve the performance of classification problem in multi-class imbalanced problem.

* * * * *

CHAPTER 3

MODULE I: METHODOLOGY FOR NIDS TO DETECT NORMAL OR ATTACK TRAFFIC

3.1 INTRODUCTION

This chapter provides the methodology for Module I (HyFSA-HEIC), which is a part of proposed NIDPS presented in Section 2.3. The purpose of this module is to detect whether the incoming network traffic is normal or attack. It is proposed to enhance the accuracy and efficiency of the NIDS as well as reduce the FPR, FNR, TBM, and TTM to work in real time. There are four main sections to portray the methodology for Module I (HyFSA-HEIC). The next section presents block diagram of Module I (HyFSA-HEIC). The third section presents the experimental setup. The experimental result and analysis is discussed in the fourth section. The summary about the chapter is presented in the last section.

3.2 BLOCK DIAGRAM OF MODULE I (HyFSA-HEIC)

This section discusses the proposed Module I named as HyFSA-HEIC (Section 2.3.2) for intelligent lightweight, accurate, and efficient anomaly based NIDS in detail. The block diagram of Module I (HyFSA-HEIC) is represented in Figure 3.1 (same as Figure 2.4). It contains following 3 phases:

Phase 1: Preprocessing of dataset

Phase 2: Selection of features using HyFSA

Phase 3: Model development using HEIC

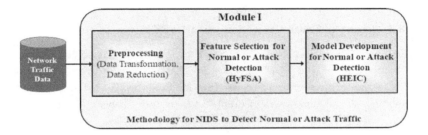

Figure 3.1: Block diagram of proposed Module I (HyFSA-HEIC)

3.3 EXPERIMENTAL SETUP

Weka is used as tool for feature selection methods, classifiers and ensembles utilized in this module. The "10% KDD" and "Corrected Test" datasets (Section 2.5) are selected for experiments. The phases defined above are followed to implement the proposed module.

3.3.1 Phase 1: Preprocessing of dataset

The "10% KDD" and "Corrected Test" datasets are preprocessed for normal or attack traffic detection. This phase contains 3 steps.

1) Data transformation: The label of each attack connection records are transformed into label "attack".

2) Data reduction: The resultant dataset contains around 70% redundant records. Therefore, these records are removed from the dataset. The resultant datasets named as "Uni KDD" and "Uni Corr" are shown in Table 2.3.

3) Creation of training and test dataset: The training ("Uni Train") and test ("Uni Test") datasets are created from "Uni KDD" by partitioning it into two equal parts, each containing 72793 records. Similarly, reduced training ("Red Uni Train") and reduced test ("Red Uni Test") datasets are created for 6 selected features in Phase 2 from "Uni Train" and "Uni Test" datasets respectively. Another test datasets "Uni Corr" and "Red Uni Corr" are also utilized for 41 and reduced 6 features respectively. Table 2.3 illustrates the detail of these datasets.

3.3.2   Phase 2: Feature Selection using HyFSA

The 6 best features are obtained out of 41 features by applying HyFSA (detail in Section 2.6) on "Uni KDD" dataset. The feature's number are {3, 5, 6, 10, 13, 29 } and their respective names are {Service, Src-bytes, Dst-bytes, Hot, Num-compromised, and Same-srv-rate} (Table 2.4 for feature number and name).

3.3.3   Phase 3: Model development using HEIC

In Module I (HyFSA-HEIC), the HEIC (Section 2.7) is employed to build the model for the normal or attack detection. This phase consists of two steps.

1) Selection of base classifiers for ensemble

The DT (C4.5), NB, NN-SGD, k-NN (k=3), RIPPER, and RF are selected as base classifiers for the ensemble (Section 2.7.2.2). These classifiers are trained on "Red Uni Train" dataset. The TPR, FPR, ACC, PRE, ROC, TBM, TTM, and RMSE are used as performance metrics in the comparisons. The results of these classifiers on training dataset using 6 features is depicted in Table 3.1. The base classifiers selected for ensemble based on performance are NB, NN-SGD, RIPPER, DT (C4.5) and RF out of 6 are employed to construct the ensemble (Section 2.7.3).

2) Step 2: Ensemble and combiner method

A parallel ensemble structure is employed to construct the heterogeneous ensemble

---

in which selected 5 classifiers—NB, NN-SGD, RIPPER, DT (C4.5) and RF are trained on "Red Uni Train" dataset (6 features) independently. Then algebraic combination rules—Average, Product, Majority Voting, Minimum, and Maximum are used to construct 5 ensembles. Table 3.2 illustrates the results of these 5 ensemble models on "Red Uni Train" dataset based on different evaluation metrics.

3.4 EXPERIMENTAL RESULTS AND ANALYSIS

Several experiments have been performed to assess the performance of Module I (HyFSA-HEIC) in terms of accuracy and efficiency. All experiments are conducted using Weka. The datasets used in the experiments for training are "Uni Train" and "Red Uni Train", and for testing are "Uni Test" , "Red Uni Test", "Uni Corr" and "Red Uni Corr". Performance metrics are used in the experiments are TPR, FPR, ACC, PRE, ROC, TBM, TTM, and RMSE. The performance of these classifiers using 6 selected features based TPR, FPR, ACC, PRE, ROC, TBM, TTM, and RMSE are evaluated on test dataset "Red Uni Test" is shown in Table 3.3. and on "Uni Corr" (41 features) and "Red Uni Corr" (6 features) in Table 3.4. The performance of 5 ensembles using 6 selected features on test dataset "Red Uni Test" is illustrated in Table 3.5 and on "Uni Corr" (41 features) and "Red Uni Corr" (6 features) in Table 3.6.

Table 3.1: Experimental results of classifiers on training dataset (6 features)

Classifiers	Evaluation Metrics							
	TPR (%)	FPR (%)	ACC (%)	PRE (%)	ROC (%)	TBM (sec)	TTM (sec)	RMSE (%)
NB	95.1	6.1	95.12	95.2	99.2	0.45	1.61	21.97
NN-SGD	97.2	3.7	97.16	97.2	96.7	170.56	1.61	16.86
k-NN(k=3)	99.9	0.1	99.87	99.9	100	0.08	5087.73	3.09
RIPPER	99.8	0.2	99.83	99.8	99.8	46.28	0.21	4.05
C4.5	99.9	0.2	99.88	99.9	100	3.24	0.35	3.32
RF	99.9	0.1	99.9	99.9	100	38.11	8.85	2.85

The training and testing are performed for 6 classifiers and 5 ensembles using 6 and 41 features. Then these classifiers and ensembles are compared using 6 features with 41 features on different evaluation metrics. Tables 2.12 and 3.1 illustrate the

Table 3.2: Experimental results of ensemble on training dataset (6 features)

Ensemble of	Evaluation Metrics							
Classifier	TPR (%)	FPR (%)	ACC (%)	PRE (%)	ROC (%)	TBM (sec)	TTM (sec)	RMSE (%)
Average	99.9	0.1	99.9	99.9	100	227.6	8.42	7.49
Product	99.6	0.5	97.16	99.6	98.3	227.12	9.91	6.14
Majority Voting	99.9	0.1	99.91	99.9	99.9	226.54	9.09	3.06
Minimum	99.6	0.5	97.16	99.6	98.3	264.01	10.39	6.14
Maximum	97.8	3.2	97.85	97.9	99.9	253.69	10.47	11.59

Table 3.3: Experimental results of classifiers on test dataset (6 features)

Classifiers	Evaluation Metrics					
	TPR(%)	FPR(%)	ACC(%)	PRE(%)	ROC(%)	RMSE(%)
NB	95.2	6.1	95.17	95.2	99.3	21.87
NN-SGD	97.2	3.6	97.23	97.3	96.8	16.64
k-NN	99.9	0.2	99.84	99.8	100	3.67
RIPPER	99.9	0.2	99.86	99.9	99.9	3.62
C4.5	99.8	0.2	99.85	99.8	99.9	3.63
RF	99.9	0.1	99.92	99.9	100	2.54

Table 3.4: Experimental results of classifiers on "Uni Corr" (41 & 6 features)

Classifiers	Evaluation Metrics & # Features											
	TPR (%)		FPR (%)		ACC (%)		PRE (%)		ROC (%)		RMSE (%)	
	41	6	41	6	41	6	41	6	41	6	41	6
NB	91.5	90.4	12.3	15	91.52	90.41	91.8	91.3	93.3	97.9	29.02	30.91
NN-SGD	92.8	91.8	10.7	12.8	92.77	91.78	93.1	92.4	91	89.5	26.88	28.67
k-NN	94.2	95.4	9	6.8	94.2	95.36	94.5	95.5	93.9	94.6	23.19	20.89
RIPPER	94.5	95.2	8.5	7.5	94.52	95.15	94.8	95.4	93.1	93.8	23.41	22.08
C4.5	94.5	92.6	8.6	11.2	94.51	92.61	94.8	93	94.6	94	23.26	25.41
RF	94.2	94.6	9.1	7.1	94.21	94.61	94.6	94.6	99.3	97.1	19.73	20.64

performances of these six classifiers trained on "Uni Train" (41 features) and "Red Uni Train" (6 features) datasets on different evaluation metrics respectively. As can be seen from Tables 2.12 and 3.1, TBM and TTM for original 41 features are remarkably higher than that of reduced 6 features. The TBM is reduced by

Table 3.5: Experimental results of ensembles on test dataset (6 features)

Ensemble of Classifier	Evaluation Metrics					
	TPR (%)	FPR (%)	ACC (%)	PRE (%)	ROC (%)	RMSE (%)
Average	99.9	0.2	99.87	99.9	100	7.5
Product	99.6	0.5	97.22	99.6	98.4	6.27
Majority Voting	99.9	0.2	99.88	99.9	99.9	3.42
Minimum	99.6	0.5	97.22	99.6	98.4	6.27
Maximum	97.8	3.2	97.84	97.9	99.9	11.6

Table 3.6: Experimental results of ensembles on "Uni Corr" (41 & 6 features)

Ensemble of Classifier	Evaluation Metrics & # Features											
	TPR (%)		FPR (%)		ACC (%)		PRE (%)		ROC (%)		RMSE (%)	
	41	6	41	6	41	6	41	6	41	6	41	6
Average	94.3	93.5	8.9	10.3	94.3	93.5	94.7	93.9	99.2	97.9	21.9	22.7
Product	93.7	93.2	9.5	11	92.7	91.1	93.9	93.8	91.7	90.3	25.2	26
Majority Voting	94.3	93.6	8.9	10.1	94.3	93.6	94.7	94	92.7	91.8	23.8	25.3
Minimum	93.7	93.2	9.5	11	92.7	91.2	93.9	93.8	91.7	90.3	25.2	26
Maximum	91	92.1	13.7	12.7	91	92.1	91.6	92.8	99	98	21.3	21.8

approximately 68-96% except for k-NN and TTM is reduced by approximately 40-94% for 6 features set. The Figures 3.4 and 3.5 show comparative graph for TBM and TTM on 41 and 6 features respectively. The performances of classifiers evaluated using test datasets "Uni Test" and "Red Uni Test" on different evaluation metrics are illustrated in Tables 2.14 and 3.3 respectively. From Figures 3.2 to 3.5, it can be observed that selection of optimized features set consume less computation time in training and testing phase and also maintain the same classification performance as of original features set.

Among 5 ensembles, ensembles using Majority Voting and Average achieved equally best performance with TPR(99.9%), FPR (0.0%), and PRE(100%) on reduced dataset. Apart from this, Majority Voting outperformed in ACC (99.91%), and Average combiner outperformed in ROC (100.0%) on reduced dataset. Majority Voting has lowest RMSE among all ensembles of 1.85% and 3.06% for 6 and 41 features respectively (Tables 3.2 and 2.13). Therefore ensemble using Majority Voting is the best performing combining rule for ensemble based on overall performance.

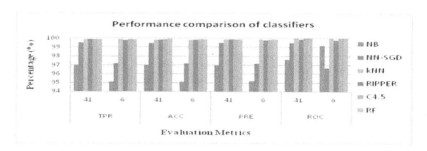

Figure 3.2: TPR, ACC, PRE & ROC of classifiers (41 & 6 features)

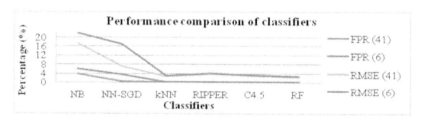

Figure 3.3: FPR & RMSE of classifiers (41 & 6 features)

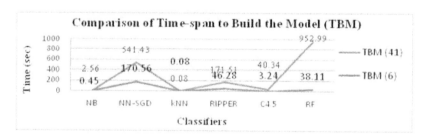

Figure 3.4: TBM (in sec) of classifiers (41 & 6 features)

It can be observed that TBM and TTM of ensembles for 6 features are drastically reduced by approximately 58-64% and 42-56 % respectively (Tables 3.2 and 2.13). The performance comparisons of ensembles for TPR, ACC, PRE, and ROC are shown in Figure 3.6, for FPR and RMSE in Figure 3.7, for TBM in Figure 3.8, and for TTM in Figure 3.9 for 41 and 6 features. The performance of classifiers and ensembles also tested on "Red Uni Corr" test dataset as shown in Tables 3.4 and 3.6 respectively are near to the performance of 41 features on all evaluation metrics.

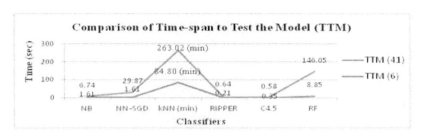

Figure 3.5: TTM (in sec & for k-NN in min) of classifiers (41 & 6 features)

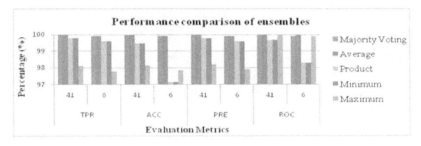

Figure 3.6: TPR, ACC, PRE & ROC of ensembles (41 & 6 features)

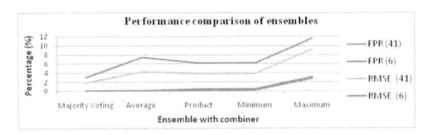

Figure 3.7: FPR & RMSE of ensemble (41 & 6 features)

Based on the comparison of results of 5 ensemble models (Tables 3.2 and 3.5) and 6 classifiers (Tables 3.1 and 3.3) on different evaluation metrics on reduced 6 features has shown that ensemble using Majority Voting outperformed other ensembles and single classifiers. Hence, it is more capable and reliable for NIDS. Therefore, it is selected as ensemble model for Module I (HyFSA-HEIC). The performance comparison of Module I (HyFSA-HEIC) with single classifiers NB,

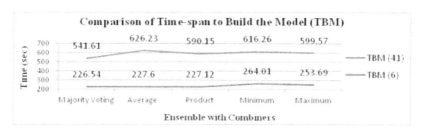

Figure 3.8: TBM (in sec) of ensembles (41 & 6 features)

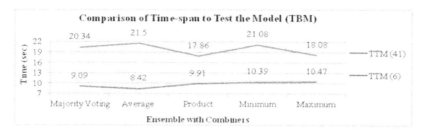

Figure 3.9: TTM (in sec) of ensembles (41 & 6 features)

NN-SGD, RIPPER, C4.5, and RF on TPR, ACC, PRE, and ROC is shown in Figure 3.10 and on FPR and RMSE in Figure 3.11. The performance of Module I (HyFSA-HEIC) has been enhanced in terms of TRP (99.9%), ACC (99.91%), PRE (99.9%), ROC (99.9%), with extremely low FPR (0.1%) and RMSE (3.06%), has faster TBM and TTM than the ensemble with full features set.

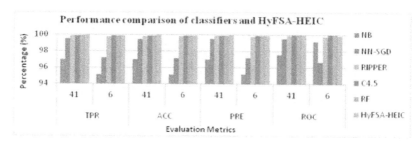

Figure 3.10: TPR, ACC, PRE, & ROC of classifiers and HyFSA-HEIC

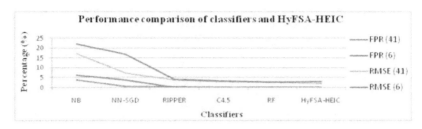

Figure 3.11: FPR & RMSE of classifiers and HyFSA-HEIC (41 & 6 features)

3.5 SUMMARY

This chapter presented the methodology for Module I (HyFSA-HEIC), which is a part of proposed NIDPS presented in Section 2.3. The purpose of this module is to detect the malicious network traffic. It is proposed to create system lightweight and increase the performance in terms of increased ACC and decreased FPR, FNR, TBM and TTM. It integrates HyFSA (Section 2.6) and HEIC (Section 2.7), in which HyFSA is employed to select optimal feature subset and HEIC to increase the performance of NIDS. The main challenging issues arise in IDS are to handle large-scale high dimensional dataset and maximizing overall ACC and less false alarm. The Module I (HyFSA-HEIC) addresses these issues by incorporating HyFSA and HEIC. It utilized 5 diverse accurate intelligent classifiers NB, NN-SGD, RIPPER, DT (C4.5) and RF and Majority Voting to produce the final decisions of these 5 classifiers using only 6 selected features i.e. only 15% of original 41 features. The results showed that Module I (HyFSA-HEIC) outperformed other methods with TPR (99.9%), ACC (99.91%), PRE (99.9%), ROC (99.9%), and low FPR (0.1%) and RMSE (3.06%) with minimum number of selected 6 features. It also reduced the TMB by 50.79% and TTM by 55.30% on reduced features set. In conclusion, integrating feature selection approach to the heterogeneous ensemble of intelligent classifier improve the TPR, ACC, PRE, and ROC and reduce the FPR, FNR and ERR with minimum computation time.

* * * * *

CHAPTER 4

MODULE II: METHODOLOGY FOR NIDS TO DETECT SPECIFIC ATTACK TYPE

4.1 INTRODUCTION

This chapter provides the methodology for Module II, which is a part of proposed NIDPS presented in Section 2.3. The purpose of this module is to further identify the type of intrusion (attack) accurately specially the rare attacks. The imbalance in network traffic data imposes poor classification for rare class data. Therefore, this module proposes an intelligent model for anomaly based NIDS that is accurate, efficient and lightweight to further identify exact type of intrusion (attack) once the intrusion is detected in network traffic. There are four main sections to portray the methodology for Module II. The next section presents block diagram of Module II. The third section describes the experimental setup. The experimental result and analysis is discussed in the fourth section. The summary about the chapter is presented in the last section.

4.2   BLOCK DIAGRAM OF MODULE II

This section presents the block diagram of proposed Module II to detect type of attack, once attack is detected in incoming network traffic. This module serially integrates HySCBA, OVR binarization technique, HyFSA and OVR multi-class classifier using HEIC for the detection of type of attack in multi-class imbalanced dataset. The block diagram of Module II is represented in Figure 4.1 (same as Figure 2.5). It consists of following 5 phases:

Phase 1: Preprocessing of dataset

Phase 2: Balance class distribution using HySCBA

Phase 3: Conversion of multi-class to binary-classes using OVR

Phase 4: Feature selection using HyFSA for each attack type

Phase 5: Model development using OVR multi-class classifier using HEIC

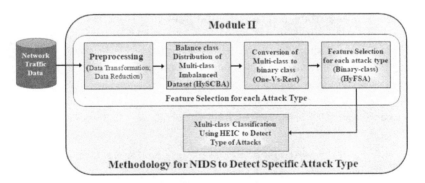

Figure 4.1: Block diagram of proposed Module II

4.3   EXPERIMENTAL SETUP

Weka is used as tool for feature selection methods and classifiers utilized in this module. The "10% KDD" dataset (Section 2.5) is selected for experiments. The phases defined above are followed to implement the proposed module.

4.3.1 Phase 1: Preprocessing of dataset

The "10% KDD" dataset is preprocessed for attack class classification (detection of specific attack type). This phase consists of 2 steps.

1) Data transformation: For attack class classification, the label of each attack connection recodrs are transformed into specific attack type (DoS, Probe, R2l, U2R) according to Table 2.2.

2) Data reduction: For attack class classification, dataset must contain only attack types, so normal connection records are removed from dataset. The resultant datasets also contains large number of duplicate records. The attack classes of "10'% KDD" dataset contains around 85'% duplicate records (Table 2.3). Since connection records of Probe, R2L and U2R are very less in numbers with comparison to DoS attack, therefore duplicate records of only DoS attack are removed. The resultant dataset named as "Atk Uni KDD" is shown in Table 4.1.

4.3.2 Phase 2: Balance class distribution using HySCBA

The hybrid based sampling algorithm, HySCBA, proposed in Section 2.8 has been employed to balance the class distribution of attack classes of "Atk Uni KDD" which is a multi-class imbalanced dataset. After applying HySCBA on dataset "Atk Uni KDD", the distribution of each attack types of obtained balanced dataset named as "Bal KDD" is depicted in Table 4.1 (detail steps in Section 2.8).

Table 4.1: Statistics of instances of each attack type

Attack Name	Datasets		
	Atk KDD	Atk Uni KDD	Bal Atk KDD
DoS	391,458	54,572	4,999
Probe	4,107	4,107	5,010
R2L	1,126	1,126	4,999
U2R	52	52	4,999
Total	**396,743**	**59,857**	**20,007**

4.3.3 Phase 3: Conversion of multi-class to binary-classes using OVR

To detect the type of attack, OVR binarization technique is employed for multi-class attack classification. There are four classes (DoS, Probe, R2L, U2R) for attack categories in datasets. Thus, 4-class classification task is decomposed into 4 binary-class classification subtasks. Then binary classifier is constructed to discriminate each class from all other classes for each subtask. In this, four training datasets are constructed from training dataset as DoS-Vs-Rest, Probe-Vs-Rest, R2L-Vs-Rest, and U2R-Vs-Rest. The distribution of each attack type is shown in Table 4.2 after performing OVR binarization technique.

Table 4.2: Statistics of each attack type after performing OVR

Binary Class Attack Name	# Instance
DoS-Vs-Rest	4,999 / 15,008
Probe-Vs-Rest	5,010 / 14,997
R2L-Vs-Rest	4,999 / 15,008
U2R-Vs-Rest	4,999 / 15,008

4.3.4 Phase 4: Feature selection using HyFSA for each attack type

The HyFSA (Section 2.6) has been employed to obtain feature subsets for each binary-class that represents each attack class obtained in Phase 3. In this, class-specific feature subset is obtained rather than one feature subset for all attack classes. Hence, four feature subsets will be produced for these four attack types by performing the steps as stated in the algorithm of proposed HyFSA (Section 2.6.1). The "Atk Uni KDD" dataset is used in feature selection and classifier NB to evaluate the different feature subsets obtained at different steps of HyFSA and also in wrapper method. The details of feature selection for DoS-Vs-Rest, Probe-Vs-Rest, R2L-Vs-Rest, and U2R-Vs-Rest are presented in the subsequent subsections.

4.3.4.1 Feature selection for DoS-Vs-Rest

The features obtained by IG and GR are ranked in descending order as depicted in Tables 4.3 and 4.4 respectively. The features {15, 20, 21} from Tables 4.3 and 4.4 have the rank 0. Hence, only 38 features are appropriate for further processing. The TPR, FPR, and RMSE obtained by classifier NB of first N (where, N=1 to 38) number of features from Tables 4.3 and 4.4 using 5-fold cross validation are shown in Table 4.5. The numbers of features selected based on performance from Table 4.5 are 9 and 18 respectively shown in bold. Therefore 9 and 18 are values of N1 and N2 at steps 4 and 5 respectively.The selected feature subsets and performance of these subsets at each step of the proposed HyFSA by classifier NB using 10-fold cross validation is depicted in Table 4.6. Finally, nine features {3, 4, 8, 23, 30, 35, 36, 37, and 38} are selected for DoS-Vs-Rest by the HyFSA.

Table 4.3: Feature number (#) and rank of features using IG for DoS-Vs-Rest

S.No	#	Rank	S.No	#	Rank	S.No	#	Rank
1	30	0.690556	15	36	0.354409	29	41	0.026898
2	23	0.681711	16	32	0.303013	30	31	0.023346
3	35	0.670149	17	12	0.247675	31	18	0.017678
4	29	0.608489	18	6	0.182364	32	2	0.01704
5	34	0.562627	19	37	0.158612	33	11	0.009602
6	4	0.533676	20	1	0.155243	34	8	0.009449
7	24	0.530984	21	10	0.128421	35	19	0.004611
8	3	0.524067	22	40	0.091763	36	9	0.003877
9	38	0.491615	23	14	0.064976	37	28	0.00195
10	25	0.483463	24	17	0.063314	38	7	0.0002
11	39	0.436585	25	13	0.05604	39	15	0
12	26	0.434755	26	27	0.044427	40	20	0
13	33	0.433758	27	16	0.030743	41	21	0
14	5	0.364416	28	22	0.030494			

Table 4.4: Feature number (#) and rank of features using GR for DoS-Vs-Rest

S.No	#	Rank	S.No	#	Rank	S.No	#	Rank
1	26	0.55254	15	34	0.20777	29	31	0.07366
2	39	0.44232	16	3	0.18938	30	18	0.07085
3	38	0.41938	17	37	0.17587	31	11	0.06111
4	29	0.40326	18	1	0.17485	32	40	0.05499
5	25	0.39166	19	6	0.16441	33	19	0.05261
6	23	0.35243	20	5	0.16351	34	9	0.05095
7	30	0.33858	21	7	0.13584	35	27	0.04171

Continue ...

105

Table 4.4 – (Continued)

S.No	#	Rank	S.No	#	Rank	S.No	#	Rank
8	4	0.31919	22	10	0.11427	36	2	0.03275
9	12	0.24852	23	14	0.10963	37	41	0.0226
10	24	0.22941	24	17	0.10842	38	28	0.00259
11	35	0.22779	25	33	0.09692	39	20	0
12	36	0.22486	26	16	0.08315	40	15	0
13	8	0.21924	27	22	0.08293	41	21	0
14	32	0.21608	28	13	0.07851			

Table 4.5: Performance of first N1 & N2 features by NB for DoS-Vs-Rest

S.No	#Feature	Performance of first N1 feature(s) from Table 4.3 (IG)			Performance of first N2 feature(s) from Table 4.4 (GR)		
		TPR(%)	FPR(%)	RMSE(%)	TPR(%)	FPR(%)	RMSE(%)
1	41	97.60	2.50	15.04	97.60	2.50	15.04
2	1	84.20	9.20	41.20	92.30	17.30	27.31
3	2	97.30	5.60	18.88	92.30	17.30	27.67
4	3	94.50	5.10	31.97	92.20	17.30	27.81
5	4	97.40	5.20	15.39	92.20	17.30	27.82
6	5	98.20	4.70	13.03	91.80	17.40	28.55
7	6	98.50	4.40	12.35	91.90	17.40	28.35
8	7	98.40	3.80	12.40	93.00	17.00	26.26
9	8	98.40	3.70	12.30	93.20	16.90	25.98
10	9	**98.70**	**3.00**	**11.19**	93.50	16.80	25.09
11	10	98.10	3.30	13.79	93.70	16.20	25.00
12	11	98.00	3.70	14.75	93.70	16.30	24.30
13	12	93.80	16.20	21.56	94.30	16.30	19.16
14	13	94.00	15.50	19.76	94.50	15.60	18.63
15	14	98.00	3.30	14.08	98.80	3.10	11.63
16	15	98.50	3.50	12.13	98.90	2.80	10.59
17	16	98.70	3.40	11.59	98.90	2.80	10.56
18	17	98.70	3.40	11.55	98.90	2.70	10.57
19	18	98.70	3.20	11.28	**98.90**	**2.70**	**10.53**
20	19	98.70	3.00	11.22	98.80	2.60	10.75

Continue ...

Table 4.5 – (*Continued*)

S.No	#Feature	Performance of first N1 feature(s) from Table 4.3 (IG)			Performance of first N2 feature(s) from Table 4.4 (GR)		
		TPR(%)	FPR(%)	RMSE(%)	TPR(%)	FPR(%)	RMSE(%)
21	20	98.70	3.00	11.43	98.80	2.60	10.94
22	21	98.60	2.90	11.67	98.80	2.60	10.94
23	22	98.60	2.90	11.67	98.70	2.50	11.24
24	23	98.30	2.90	12.70	98.50	2.40	12.02
25	24	98.20	2.90	13.17	98.40	2.30	12.40
26	25	98.20	2.90	13.48	98.30	2.50	12.74
27	26	98.20	2.90	13.48	98.20	2.50	13.25
28	27	98.00	2.90	13.91	98.20	2.50	13.48
29	28	98.00	2.90	14.13	98.10	2.50	13.69
30	29	98.00	2.90	14.12	98.10	2.50	13.61
31	30	98.00	2.90	14.06	98.00	2.40	13.96
32	31	97.90	2.80	14.39	98.00	2.40	14.06
33	32	97.90	2.90	14.44	98.00	2.40	14.06
34	33	97.80	2.80	14.54	97.90	2.40	14.41
35	34	98.00	2.40	14.10	97.70	2.50	14.94
36	35	97.90	2.40	14.46	97.70	2.50	14.96
37	36	97.60	2.50	15.03	97.60	2.50	15.01
38	37	97.60	2.50	15.04	97.60	2.50	15.03
39	38	97.60	2.50	15.04	97.60	2.50	15.04

Table 4.6: Performance and feature sets stepwise by HyFSA for DoS-Vs-Rest

Steps	Feature Set	Methods	#Feature	Selected Features	TPR (%)	FPR (%)	RMSE (%)	Build (sec)
1	All	-	41	-	97.80	2.40	14.59	0.15
2	F_{CFS}	CFS+ BestFirst	8	6,8,23,24,26,29,30,39	97.90	2.70	14.12	0.02
3	F_{CON}	CON+ BestFirst	5	3,4,5,30,36	94.60	3.40	20.96	0.02

Continue ...

Table 4.6 – (*Continued*)

Steps	Feature Set	Methods	#Feature	Selected Features	TPR (%)	FPR (%)	RMSE (%)	Build (sec)
4	$F_{IG(38)}$	IG+Ranker	38	1,2,3,4,5,6,7,8,9,10,11,12, 13,14, 16,17,18,19,22,23,24, 25,26,27,28,29,30,31,32,33, 34,35,36,37, 38,39,40,41	97.80	2.40	14.59	0.11
4	$F_{IG(9)}$	IG+Ranker	9	3,4,23,24,29,30,34,35,38	98.70	3.00	11.19	0.03
5	$F_{GR(38)}$	GR+Ranker	38	1,2,3,4,5,6,7,8,9,10,11,12, 13,14,16,17,18,19,22,23,24, 25,26,27,28,29,30,31,32,33, 34,35,36,37, 38,39,40,41	97.80	2.40	14.59	0.11
5	$F_{GR(18)}$	GR+Ranker	18	1,3,4,8,12,23,24,25,26,29, 30,32,34,35,36,37,38,39	98.90	2.60	10.60	0.05
6	$F_{CFS \cap CON}$	-	1	30	95.90	5.80	41.23	0.01
6	$F_{IG(9)} \cap GR(18)$	-	9	3,4,23,24,29,30,34,35,38	98.70	3.00	11.19	0.03
7	F_{IniFea}	-	1	30	95.90	5.80	41.23	0.01
8	$F_{\cup}$	-	20	1,3,4,5,6,8,12,23,24,25,26, 29,30,32,34,35,36,37,38,39	98.80	2.60	11.01	0.06
8	F_{Left}	-	19	1,3,4,5,6,8,12,23,24,25,26, 29,32,34,35,36,37,38,39	98.30	2.70	12.83	0.07
9	F_{Temp}	Wrapper+ LFS+NB	9	3,4,8,23,30,35,36,37,38	99.20	1.90	8.68	0.03
10	F_{Final}	**HyFSA**	**9**	**3,4,8,23,30,35,36,37,38**	**99.20**	**1.90**	**8.68**	**0.03**

4.3.4.2   Feature selection for Probe-Vs-Rest

The features obtained by IG and GR are ranked in descending order as depicted in Tables 4.7 and 4.8 respectively. The features {7, 15, 20, 21} from Tables 4.7 and 4.8 have the rank 0. Hence, only 37 features are appropriate for further processing. The TPR, FPR, and RMSE obtained by classifier NB of first N (where, N=1 to 37) number of features from Tables 4.7 and 4.8 using 5-fold cross validation are shown in Table 4.9. The numbers of features selected based on performance from Table 4.9 are 2 and 20 respectively shown in bold. Therefore 2 and 20 are values of N1 and N2 at steps 4 and 5 respectively. The selected feature subsets and performance of these subsets at each step by the proposed HyFSA by classifier NB using 10-fold cross validation is shown in Table 4.10. Finally, six features {2, 3, 4, 29, 34, and 35} are selected for Probe-Vs-Rest by the HyFSA.

Table 4.7: Feature number (#) and rank of features using IG for Probe-Vs-Rest

S.No	#	Rank	S.No	#	Rank	S.No	#	Rank
1	3	0.45471	15	25	0.1972	29	36	0.04182
2	35	0.43241	16	28	0.18471	30	26	0.03579
3	33	0.39012	17	6	0.17415	31	16	0.03082
4	5	0.38788	18	2	0.16137	32	22	0.03057
5	34	0.31796	19	38	0.15113	33	18	0.01772
6	30	0.27878	20	24	0.13499	34	11	0.00963
7	12	0.27215	21	32	0.13094	35	19	0.00462
8	23	0.26589	22	10	0.1303	36	9	0.00389
9	27	0.25985	23	1	0.12679	37	8	0.00196
10	4	0.25433	24	31	0.11541	38	7	0
11	40	0.24347	25	14	0.06514	39	15	0
12	29	0.22954	26	17	0.06348	40	20	0
13	41	0.21717	27	13	0.06167	41	21	0
14	37	0.21207	28	39	0.05747			

Table 4.8: Feature number(#) and rank of features using GR for Probe-Vs-Rest

S.No	#	Rank	S.No	#	Rank	S.No	#	Rank
1	2	0.3101	15	25	0.1551	29	24	0.0673
2	31	0.2972	16	4	0.1521	30	11	0.0613
3	12	0.2731	17	37	0.1392	31	39	0.0572
4	28	0.2592	18	40	0.131	32	19	0.0527
5	27	0.2564	19	29	0.1293	33	9	0.0511
6	35	0.2264	20	23	0.1124	34	32	0.0503
7	5	0.2064	21	14	0.1099	35	26	0.0475
8	41	0.1931	22	17	0.1087	36	8	0.0455
9	30	0.1728	23	13	0.1074	37	36	0.0244

Continue ...

Table 4.8 – (*Continued*)

S.No	#	Rank	S.No	#	Rank	S.No	#	Rank
10	6	0.1669	24	38	0.0988	38	15	0
11	3	0.1643	25	16	0.0834	39	7	0
12	33	0.1631	26	1	0.0832	40	20	0
13	34	0.1587	27	22	0.0831	41	21	0
14	10	0.1554	28	18	0.071			

Table 4.9: Performance of first N1 & N2 features by NB for Probe-Vs-Rest

S.No	#Feature	Performance of first N1 feature(s) from Table 4.7 (IG)			Performance of first N2 feature(s) from Table 4.8 (GR)		
		TPR(%)	FPR(%)	RMSE(%)	TPR(%)	FPR(%)	RMSE(%)
1	41	84.40	5.40	37.41	84.40	5.40	37.41
2	1	89.20	25.60	28.56	83.00	48.80	37.44
3	2	**97.50**	**4.00**	**3.94**	81.50	52.30	41.52
4	3	97.00	4.10	16.56	82.70	48.80	33.55
5	4	90.80	6.20	29.21	91.50	8.20	28.63
6	5	90.90	6.10	29.58	91.80	8.40	27.35
7	6	88.70	10.60	29.58	91.30	10.30	27.77
8	7	93.60	4.00	24.78	87.40	10.40	31.09
9	8	93.60	4.10	25.15	87.40	10.40	31.09
10	9	90.60	8.00	27.61	91.80	8.70	28.83
11	10	88.70	9.60	28.61	87.60	9.20	33.47
12	11	89.70	10.50	29.74	89.30	4.50	32.47
13	12	89.50	10.60	30.31	89.20	4.30	32.57
14	13	90.10	11.10	29.57	89.20	4.20	32.62
15	14	93.40	5.20	25.47	74.20	8.70	40.65
16	15	93.20	5.00	25.24	92.70	2.60	27.09
17	16	92.90	5.40	26.45	92.70	2.60	26.66
18	17	93.10	3.50	26.14	92.70	2.60	26.12
19	18	93.20	3.10	25.93	93.00	2.60	25.07
20	19	93.30	2.80	25.87	93.20	2.50	24.88
21	20	93.30	3.00	25.86	**94.20**	**2.40**	**24.19**
22	21	93.30	2.90	25.87	88.90	3.80	31.06

Continue ...

Table 4.9 – (*Continued*)

S.No	#Feature	Performance of first N1 feature(s) from Table 4.7 (IG)			Performance of first N2 feature(s) from Table 4.8 (GR)		
		TPR(%)	FPR(%)	RMSE(%)	TPR(%)	FPR(%)	RMSE(%)
23	22	92.90	2.70	26.32	88.50	3.90	33.90
24	23	92.90	2.70	25.87	75.10	8.40	44.77
25	24	93.70	2.70	24.30	91.40	2.90	28.79
26	25	92.70	2.70	26.83	88.20	4.00	33.74
27	26	92.50	2.70	27.28	88.30	4.00	32.93
28	27	91.70	2.90	28.35	88.20	4.00	34.20
29	28	92.20	2.80	27.77	82.10	6.00	39.69
30	29	92.20	2.80	27.82	79.70	7.00	41.42
31	30	92.20	2.80	27.88	74.90	8.50	48.11
32	31	92.20	2.80	27.94	86.70	4.60	35.45
33	32	92.20	2.80	27.95	77.70	7.60	43.72
34	33	88.60	4.00	31.78	73.80	8.90	49.18
35	34	89.10	3.80	32.74	73.60	9.00	49.60
36	35	89.00	3.80	33.39	82.60	6.00	38.63
37	36	84.40	5.40	37.41	82.60	6.00	38.63
38	37	84.40	5.40	37.41	84.40	5.40	37.41

Table 4.10: Performance and feature sets stepwise by HyFSA for Probe-Vs-Rest

Steps	Feature Set	Methods	#Feature	Selected Features	TPR (%)	FPR (%)	RMSE (%)	Build (sec)
1	All	-	41	-	80.40	6.70	39.46	0.29
2	F_{CFS}	CFS+ BestFirst	7	2,6,12,27,31,33,35	71.60	9.60	45.91	0.03
3	F_{CON}	CON+ BestFirst	6	1,4,5,23,35,40	84.50	29.00	37.45	0.07
4	$F_{IG(37)}$	IG+Ranker	37	1,2,3,4,5,6,8,9,10,11, 12,13,14,16,17,18,19, 22,23,24,25,26,27,28, 29,30,31,32,33,34,35, 36,37,38,39,40,41	80.40	6.70	39.46	0.1

Continue ...

Table 4.10 – (*Continued*)

Steps	Feature Set	Methods	#Feature	Selected Features	TPR (%)	FPR (%)	RMSE (%)	Build (sec)
4	$F_{IG(2)}$	IG+Ranker	2	3,35	97.50	4.00	15.44	0.01
5	$F_{GR(37)}$	GR+Ranker	37	1,2,3,4,5,6,8,9,10,11, 12,13,14,16,17,18,19, 22,23,24,25,26,27,28, 29,30,31,32,33,34,35, 36,37,38,39,40,41	80.40	6.70	39.46	0.09
5	$F_{GR(20)}$	GR+Ranker	20	2,3,4,5,6,10,12,23,25, 27,28,29,30,31,33,34, 35,37,40,41	94.40	2.30	23.80	0.06
6	F_{CFS} $\cap CON$	-	1	35	89.30	27.10	31.64	0.01
6	$F_{IG(2)}$ $\cap GR(20)$	-	2	3, 35	97.50	4.00	15.44	0.01
7	F_{IniFea}	-	1	35	89.30	27.10	31.64	0.01
8	$F_{\cup}$	-	21	1,2,3,4,5,6,10,12,23, 25,27,28,29,30,31, 33,34,35,37,40,41	94.50	2.30	23.35	0.06
8	F_{Left}	-	20	1,2,3,4,5,6,10,12,23, 25,27,28,29,30,31, 33,34,37,40, 41	92.10	4.50	26.18	0.06
9	F_{Temp}	Wrapper+ LFS+NB	6	2,3,4,29,34,35	98.10	2.30	14.15	0.01
10	F_{Final}	**HyFSA**	**6**	**2,3,4,29,34,35**	**98.10**	**2.30**	**14.15**	**0.01**

4.3.4.3 Feature selection for R2L-Vs-Rest

The features obtained by IG and GR are ranked in descending order as depicted in Tables 4.11 and 4.12 respectively. The features {7, 20, 21} from Tables 4.11 and 4.12 have the rank 0. Hence, only 38 features are appropriate for further processing. The TPR, FPR, and RMSE obtained by classifier NB of first N (where, N=1 to 38) number of features from Tables 4.11 and 4.12 using 5-fold cross validation are shown in Table 4.13. The numbers of features selected based on performance from

112

Table 4.13 are 34 and 26 respectively shown in bold. Therefore 34 and 26 are values of N1 and N2 at steps 4 and 5 respectively. The selected feature subsets and performance of these subsets at each step by the proposed HyFSA by classifier NB using 10-fold cross validation is shown in Table 4.14. Finally, six features {1, 3, 4, 5, 22, and 30} are selected for R2L-Vs-Rest by the HyFSA.

Table 4.11: Feature number (#) and rank of features using IG for R2L-Vs-Rest

S.No	#	Rank	S.No	#	Rank	S.No	#	Rank
1	5	0.715273	15	10	0.179706	29	28	0.044824
2	3	0.560633	16	32	0.17666	30	2	0.042571
3	33	0.282686	17	39	0.158758	31	31	0.030227
4	35	0.257696	18	22	0.153254	32	16	0.027404
5	6	0.249526	19	25	0.137503	33	11	0.025955
6	12	0.245651	20	40	0.137417	34	18	0.011646
7	34	0.239636	21	38	0.122945	35	19	0.002414
8	23	0.232307	22	41	0.119341	36	8	0.001954
9	4	0.222489	23	36	0.107157	37	9	0.001499
10	29	0.211666	24	26	0.101141	38	15	0.0005
11	1	0.209354	25	27	0.058932	39	7	0
12	30	0.209216	26	13	0.058511	40	20	0
13	37	0.203435	27	14	0.052201	41	21	0
14	24	0.180774	28	17	0.048585			

Table 4.12: Feature number(#) and rank of features using GR for R2L-Vs- Rest

S.No	#	Rank	S.No	#	Rank	S.No	#	Rank
1	22	0.4168	15	26	0.1268	29	31	0.0766
2	5	0.2904	16	10	0.1194	30	16	0.0727
3	12	0.2188	17	25	0.1118	31	38	0.0726
4	3	0.2026	18	41	0.109	32	28	0.0629
5	29	0.1741	19	37	0.1086	33	32	0.0605
6	19	0.1579	20	13	0.1006	34	27	0.0545
7	23	0.157	21	35	0.092	35	18	0.0467
8	39	0.1493	22	24	0.0902	36	36	0.0456

Continue ...

Table 4.12 – (*Continued*)

S.No	#	Rank	S.No	#	Rank	S.No	#	Rank
9	15	0.1493	23	14	0.0882	37	8	0.0453
10	11	0.1442	24	34	0.0855	38	9	0.0197
11	1	0.1389	25	17	0.0828	39	7	0
12	30	0.1359	26	2	0.0818	40	20	0
13	4	0.1331	27	40	0.0816	41	21	0
14	6	0.1284	28	33	0.0805			

Table 4.13: Performance of first N1 & N2 features by NB for R2L-Vs-Rest

S.No	#Feature	Performance of first N1 feature(s) from Table 4.11			Performance of first N2 feature(s) from Table 4.12		
		TPR(%)	FPR(%)	RMSE(%)	TPR(%)	FPR(%)	RMSE(%)
1	41	89.5	5.7	32.06	89.5	5.7	32.06
2	1	34.1	37.4	57.17	82.1	53.9	41.86
3	2	88.6	22.1	33.02	82.3	53.1	40.45
4	3	88.5	22.4	33.41	82.3	53.1	36.78
5	4	76.1	25.1	41.45	90.0	19.7	30.10
6	5	87.0	26.0	34.60	80.2	22.6	36.50
7	6	86.9	25.3	34.85	80.3	22.5	35.15
8	7	86.9	25.0	36.01	83.0	9.7	40.37
9	8	82.3	11.7	40.79	80.4	9.4	42.15
10	9	82.9	9.6	40.42	80.4	9.5	42.15
11	10	82.7	7.9	40.50	83.0	7.0	40.96
12	11	82.7	7.9	40.51	83.0	7.0	40.96
13	12	82.6	7.6	41.27	80.7	7.8	42.53
14	13	82.7	7.6	40.80	80.8	7.7	43.00
15	14	81.9	8.0	41.58	83.5	8.7	39.59
16	15	83.3	7.7	40.32	83.5	6.8	40.32
17	16	83.2	7.7	40.40	82.7	10.8	40.20
18	17	81.9	8.1	41.62	82.3	7.5	41.12
19	18	83.6	8.2	39.81	81.9	7.3	41.77
20	19	82.9	8.0	40.78	82.0	7.4	41.61
21	20	81.7	10.5	42.16	82.1	7.5	41.62

Continue . . .

Table 4.13 – (*Continued*)

S.No	#Feature	Performance of first N1 feature(s) from Table 4.11			Performance of first N2 feature(s) from Table 4.12		
		TPR(%)	FPR(%)	RMSE(%)	TPR(%)	FPR(%)	RMSE(%)
22	21	80.3	11.0	43.34	82.4	7.7	41.42
23	22	79.8	11.1	44.26	82.2	7.6	41.91
24	23	79.8	11.1	44.22	90.3	5.1	30.23
25	24	78.5	11.6	45.55	90.2	5.1	30.27
26	25	78.2	11.7	46.07	90.3	5.1	29.87
27	26	78.2	11.7	46.02	**90.8**	**4.9**	**29.52**
28	27	87.3	9.0	34.99	90.6	5.0	30.01
29	28	87.4	9.0	34.76	90.6	5.0	30.00
30	29	87.1	9.1	35.29	90.3	5.4	30.72
31	30	88.5	8.6	33.49	90.2	5.5	30.89
32	31	88.3	9.0	33.81	89.9	5.6	31.55
33	32	88.2	9.0	33.94	89.8	5.6	31.78
34	33	89.5	5.7	32.05	89.7	5.6	31.84
35	34	**89.5**	**5.7**	**32.04**	89.4	5.7	32.12
36	35	89.5	5.7	32.05	89.5	5.7	32.02
37	36	89.5	5.7	32.05	89.5	5.7	32.05
38	37	89.5	5.7	32.06	89.5	5.7	32.05
39	38	89.5	5.7	32.06	89.5	5.7	32.06

Table 4.14: Performance and feature sets stepwise by HyFSA for R2L-Vs-Rest

Steps	Feature Set	Methods	#Feature	Selected Features	TPR (%)	FPR (%)	RMSE (%)	Build (sec)
1	All	-	41	-	89.4	5.7	32.28	0.13
2	F_{CFS}	CFS+ BestFirst	5	3,5,19,22,29	92.2	13.5	27.07	0.02
3	F_{CON}	CON+ BestFirst	7	3,5,6,10,13,22,32	81.7	53.2	42.67	0.02

Continue ...

Table 4.14 – (*Continued*)

Steps	Feature Set	Methods	#Feature	Selected Features	TPR (%)	FPR (%)	RMSE (%)	Build (sec)
4	$F_{IG(38)}$	IG+Ranker	38	1,2,3,4,5,6,8,9,10,11,12,13, 14,15,16,17,18,19,22,23,24, 25,26,27,28,29,30,31,32,33, 34,35,36,37,38,39,40,41	89.4	5.7	32.38	0.1
4	$F_{IG(34)}$	IG+Ranker	34	1,2,3,4,5,6,10,11,12,13,14,16, 17,18,22,23,24,25,26,27,28,29, 30,31,32,33,34,35,36,37,38,39, 40,41	89.4	5.7	32.25	0.1
5	$F_{GR(38)}$	GR+Ranker	38	1,2,3,4,5,6,8,9,10,11,12,13,14, 15,16,17,18,19,22,23,24,25,26, 27,28,29,30,31,32,33,34,35,36, 37,38,39,40,41	89.4	5.7	32.28	0.1
5	$F_{GR(26)}$	GR+Ranker	26	1,2,3,4,5,6,10,11,12,13,14,15, 17,19,22,23,24,25,26,29,30,34, 35,37,39,41	90.6	5.0	29.80	0.07
6	$F_{CFS \cap CON}$	-	3	3,5,22	82.2	53.2	32.35	0.01
6	$F_{IG(34) \cap GR(26)}$	-	24	1,2,3,4,5,6,10,11,12,13,14,17, 22,23,24,25,26,29,30,34,35, 37,39,41	90.4	5.0	29.96	0.07
7	F_{IniFea}	-	3	3,5,22	82.2	53.2	32.35	0.01
8	$F_{\cup}$	-	36	1,2,3,4,5,6,10,11,12,13,14,15, 16,17,18,19,22,23,24,25,26,27, 28,29,30,31,32,33,34,35,36,37, 38,39,40,41	89.4	5.7	32.27	0.09
8	F_{Left}	-	33	1,2,4,6,10,11,12,13,14,15,16, 17,18,19,23,24,25,26,27,28,29, 30,31,32,33,34,35,36,37,38,39, 40,41	88.7	6.0	33.43	0.12
9	F_{Temp}	Wrapper+ LFS+NB	6	1,3,4,5,22,30	93.2	12.1	25.06	0.03
10	F_{Final}	**HyFSA**	**6**	**1,3,4,5,22,30**	**93.2**	**12.1**	**25.06**	**0.03**

116

4.3.4.4 Feature selection for U2R-Vs-Rest

The features obtained by IG and GR are ranked in descending order as depicted in Tables 4.15 and 4.16 respectively. The features {7, 15, 20, 21} from Tables 4.15 and 4.16) have the rank 0. Hence, only 37 features are appropriate for further processing. The TPR, FPR, and RMSE obtained by classifier NB of first N (where, N=1 to 37) number of features from Tables 4.15 and 4.16 using 5-fold cross validation are shown in Table 4.17. The numbers of features selected based on performance from Table 4.17 are 24 and 8 respectively shown in bold. Therefore 24 and 8 are values of N1 and N2 at steps 4 and 5 respectively. The selected feature subsets and performance of these subsets at each step by the proposed HyFSA by classifier NB using 10-fold cross validation is shown in Table 4.18. Finally, nine important features {1, 3, 4, 6, 13, 14, 16, 18, and 37} are selected for U2R-Vs-Rest by the HyFSA.

Table 4.15: Feature number (#) and rank of features using IG for U2R-Vs-Rest

S.No	#	Rank	S.No	#	Rank	S.No	#	Rank
1	6	0.74979	15	34	0.23076	29	28	0.09211
2	5	0.53613	16	23	0.22414	30	18	0.07718
3	3	0.48781	17	24	0.20626	31	2	0.04156
4	1	0.47706	18	30	0.20461	32	22	0.03049
5	33	0.39014	19	29	0.20236	33	31	0.02813
6	10	0.35023	20	38	0.17951	34	11	0.02359
7	14	0.32549	21	41	0.16301	35	9	0.01433
8	17	0.31065	22	40	0.15139	36	19	0.01158
9	13	0.29902	23	16	0.14561	37	8	0.00195
10	32	0.29801	24	37	0.13736	38	20	0
11	35	0.29444	25	25	0.12987	39	7	0
12	36	0.28771	26	39	0.12074	40	15	0
13	12	0.23262	27	27	0.10995	41	21	0
14	4	0.23216	28	26	0.1044			

Table 4.16: Feature number (#) and rank of features using GR for U2R-Vs-Rest

S.No	#	Rank	S.No	#	Rank	S.No	#	Rank
1	14	0.5492	15	4	0.1389	29	40	0.0975
2	17	0.5296	16	26	0.1379	30	23	0.0967
3	13	0.4146	17	11	0.1311	31	30	0.0954
4	16	0.3865	18	36	0.1278	32	22	0.0829
5	6	0.3793	19	27	0.127	33	31	0.0809
6	18	0.3093	20	19	0.1236	34	2	0.0799
7	1	0.2904	21	28	0.1235	35	34	0.0741
8	10	0.22	22	39	0.1159	36	37	0.0702
9	12	0.2061	23	24	0.1118	37	8	0.0453
10	38	0.1941	24	29	0.1096	38	20	0
11	9	0.1883	25	35	0.1067	39	15	0
12	3	0.1763	26	33	0.103	40	7	0
13	5	0.1737	27	25	0.1019	41	21	0
14	41	0.1437	28	32	0.0979			

Table 4.17: Performance of first N1 & N2 features by NB for U2R-Vs-Rest

S.No	#Feature	Performance of first N1 feature(s) from Table 4.15 (IG)			Performance of first N2 feature(s) from Table 4.16 (GR)		
		TPR(%)	FPR(%)	RMSE(%)	TPR(%)	FPR(%)	RMSE(%)
1	41	83.9	6.0	40.09	83.9	6.0	40.09
2	1	24.8	26.6	81.02	88.5	34.0	33.28
3	2	26.3	25.5	85.80	90.6	27.4	29.96
4	3	49.8	17.5	69.96	90.9	26.7	29.68
5	4	27.3	25.5	83.48	90.7	27.2	29.79
6	5	35.6	22.6	79.18	92.0	23.2	26.59
7	6	39.2	21.4	77.55	91.1	26.0	29.06
8	7	40.3	20.8	74.17	92.3	22.4	25.74
9	8	41.0	20.1	67.77	**92.8**	**19.8**	**26.11**
10	9	64.3	12.1	61.02	90.1	12.1	27.33
11	10	69.1	10.5	54.62	65.4	11.7	54.15
12	11	77.5	7.7	47.49	69.1	11.0	47.03

Continue ...

Table 4.17 – (*Continued*)

S.No	#Feature	Performance of first N1 feature(s) from Table 4.15 (IG)			Performance of first N2 feature(s) from Table 4.16 (GR)		
		TPR(%)	FPR(%)	RMSE(%)	TPR(%)	FPR(%)	RMSE(%)
13	12	78.2	7.4	46.65	83.4	6.8	39.15
14	13	76.9	7.0	43.05	81.9	6.1	43.33
15	14	81.7	6.2	41.94	76.1	8.1	45.94
16	15	81.4	6.3	42.41	76.1	8.1	47.25
17	16	80.6	6.8	43.67	76.1	8.1	48.82
18	17	81.9	6.3	42.51	76.1	8.1	48.83
19	18	81.9	6.3	42.50	76.1	8.1	48.83
20	19	81.9	6.4	42.52	76.3	8.0	48.72
21	20	83.6	5.7	40.36	76.2	8.0	48.73
22	21	83.8	5.7	40.19	76.2	8.2	48.79
23	22	83.8	5.7	40.18	76.1	8.4	48.83
24	23	83.8	5.7	40.17	82.0	6.4	42.35
25	24	**83.9**	**5.6**	**40.15**	82.1	6.4	42.31
26	25	83.8	5.8	40.27	82.2	6.3	42.20
27	26	83.6	6.0	40.46	83.5	5.9	40.53
28	27	83.5	6.0	40.51	83.5	6.0	40.61
29	28	83.5	6.0	40.63	83.5	6.0	40.61
30	29	83.4	6.2	40.74	83.5	6.0	40.63
31	30	83.4	6.2	40.73	83.4	6.2	40.73
32	31	83.5	6.2	40.60	83.4	6.2	40.73
33	32	83.5	6.2	40.61	83.4	6.2	40.70
34	33	83.9	6.0	40.10	83.9	6.0	40.16
35	34	83.9	6.0	40.10	83.9	6.0	40.12
36	35	83.9	6.0	40.08	83.9	6.0	40.09
37	36	83.9	6.0	40.09	83.9	6.0	40.09
38	37	83.9	6.0	40.09	83.9	6.0	40.09

Table 4.18: Performance and feature sets stepwise by HyFSA for U2R-Vs-Rest

Steps	Feature Set	Methods	#Feature	Selected Features	TPR (%)	FPR (%)	RMSE (%)	Build (sec)
1	All	-	41	-	83.9	5.9	40.09	0.15
2	F_{CFS}	CFS+ BestFirst	10	1,6,8,13,14,16,17,27,31,38	77.8	7.5	47.08	0.04
3	F_{CON}	CON+ BestFirst	7	1,3,5,6,13,33,35	51.4	16.8	68.62	0.03
4	$F_{IG(37)}$	IG+Ranker	37	1,2,3,4,5,6,8,9,10,11,12,13, 14,16,17,18,19,22,23,24,25, 26,27,28,29,30,31,32,33,34, 35,36,37,38,39,40,41	83.9	5.9	40.09	0.1
4	$F_{IG(24)}$	IG+Ranker	24	1,3,4,5,6,10,12,13,14,16,17, 23,24,29,30,32,33,34,35,36, 37, 38,40,41	83.8	5.6	40.16	0.07
5	$F_{GR(37)}$	GR+Ranker	37	1,2,3,4,5,6,8,9,10,11,12,13, 14,16,17, 18,19,22,23,24,25, 26,27,28,29,30,31,32,33,34, 35,36,37,38,39,40,41	83.9	5.9	40.09	0.11
5	$F_{GR(8)}$	GR+Ranker	8	1,6,10,13,14,16,17,18	92.8	19.7	26.06	0.04
6	$F_{CFS} \cap CON$	-	3	1,6,13	27.0	25.2	84.37	0.01
6	$F_{IG(24)} \cap GR(8)$	-	7	1,6,10,13,14,16,17	34.1	22.2	58.82	0.02
7	F_{IniFea}	-	3	1,6,13	27.0	25.2	84.37	0.01
8	$F_{\cup}$	-	28	1,3,4,5,6,8,10,12,13,14,16, 17,18,23,24,27,29,30,31,32, 33,34,35,36,37, 38,40,41	84.2	5.5	39.75	0.08
8	F_{Left}	-	25	3,4,5,8,10,12,14,16,17,18, 23,24,27,29,30,31,32,33, 34,35,36,37,38,40,41	84.3	5.4	39.57	0.07
9	F_{Temp}	Wrapper+ LFS+NB	9	1,3,4,6,13,14,16,18,37	94.0	17.2	21.83	0.02
10	F_{Final}	**HyFSA**	**9**	**1,3,4,6,13,14,16,18,37**	**94.0**	**17.2**	**21.83**	**0.02**

4.3.4.5 Creation of single feature set

The final optimal feature sets for each attack type are summarized in Table 4.19. These four feature sets are combined to obtain single feature set for the detection of type of attack. It contains 20 features {1, 2, 3, 4, 5, 6, 8, 13, 14, 16, 18, 22, 23, 29, 30, 34, 35, 36, 37, and 38}, which consist of features of each attack type, is shown in Table 4.19. The resultant dataset is named as "Com Red KDD".

Table 4.19: Statistics, # features and selected features of each attack type

Attack Name	#Instance	# Features	Selected Features
DoS-Vs-Rest	4999 / 15008	9	3,4,8,23,30,35,36,37,38
Probe-Vs-Rest	5010 / 14997	6	2,3,4,29,34,35
R2L-Vs-Rest	4999 / 15008	6	1,3,4,5,22,30
U2R-Vs-Rest	4999 / 15008	9	1,3,4,6,13,14,16,18,37
Combined features from 4 feature subsets		20	1,2,3,4,5,6,8,13,14,16,18,22, 23,29,30,34,35,36,37,38

4.3.5 Phase 5: Model development using OVR multi-class classifier using HEIC

The multi-class classifier is the simplest way to handle dataset with more than two classes. Many machine learning techniques can deal with multiple classes, but has risk to bias towards majority classes. Therefore, class binarization technique is used to decompose multi-class problem into several binary-class problems. These binary class problems are solved individually and then their results are combined to predict the final result.

The multi-class classification using OVR binarization technique is employed to detect the type of attack class. In this, OVR binarization technique decomposes 4 categories of attack classes (DoS, Probe, R2L and U2R) into 4 binary-class classification problems. Each binary-class classification problem is handled by binary classifier, which distinguishes each class from rest of the classes. Whole training dataset is used in learning phase of the classifiers in which connection records from the single class are considered as positive class and rest other connection records as negative class. The HEIC (detail in Section 2.7) is employed as a binary classifier. For 4-class classification, a set of 4 HEIC classifiers are constructed and each HEIC is trained to separate one class from the rest. At the time of prediction, the test instance is submitted to all binary classifiers. If precisely, only one classifier gives a positive output, then corresponding class is predicted as final prediction of multi-class classification. In other cases, if more than one classifier predicts positive output then confidence of the classifiers is used to decide the final output. The class of the corresponding classifier which has the largest confidence is predicted as output. If the largest confidence is not unique then random tie-breaking is applied in which one class is randomly selected among the set of predicted classes.

The OVR multi-class HEIC classifier is built employing "Com Red KDD" dataset using 10-fold cross validation for the detection of type of attack class. It is also built by using "Atk Uni KDD" and "Bal KDD" datasets using 10-fold cross validation for comparison. Performance metrics used in the experiments are TPR, FPR, TNR, GM, TBM, PRE, FI-S, ROC, and PRC. The result is depicted in Table 4.20.

Table 4.20: Experimental results of OVR multi-class HEIC on training datasets

Evaluation	Attack	Dataset (# Feature)		
Metrics	Name	Atk Uni KDD (41)	Bal KDD (41)	Com Red KDD (20)
TPR	U2R	90.4	100.0	100.0
	DoS	100.0	100.0	100.0
	R2L	99.2	99.7	99.6
	Probe	99.8	100.0	99.9
FPR	U2R	0.0	0.1	0.1
	DoS	0.2	0.0	0.0
	R2L	0.0	0.0	0.0
	Probe	0.0	0.1	0.1
TNR	U2R	100.0	99.9	99.9
	DoS	99.8	100.0	100.0
	R2L	100.0	100.0	100.0
	Probe	100.0	99.9	99.9
GM	U2R	95.1	99.9	99.9
	DoS	99.9	100.0	100.0
	R2L	99.6	99.8	99.8

Continue ...

Table 4.20 – (*Continued*)

Evaluation Metrics	Attack Name	Dataset (# Feature)		
		Atk Uni KDD (41)	Bal KDD (41)	Com Red KDD (20)
	Probe	99.9	99.9	99.9
TBM (Sec.)	-	257.15	95.67	51.12
PRE	U2R	87.0	99.8	99.6
	DoS	100.0	100.0	100.0
	R2L	99.9	100.0	100.0
	Probe	99.9	99.8	99.8
F1-S	U2R	88.7	99.9	99.8
	DoS	100.0	100.0	100.0
	R2L	99.6	99.8	99.8
	Probe	99.9	99.9	99.8
ROC	U2R	97.1	100.0	100.0
	DoS	100.0	100.0	100.0
	R2L	99.8	99.9	99.9
	Probe	100.0	100.0	100.0
PRC	U2R	85.2	99.9	99.9
	DoS	100.0	100.0	100.0
	R2L	99.6	99.9	99.9
	Probe	99.8	99.9	100.0

4.4 EXPERIMENTAL RESULTS AND ANALYSIS

Several experiments have been performed to evaluate the performance of Module II in terms of accuracy and efficiency. All experiments are conducted using Weka. Datasets used in the experiments are "Atk Uni KDD", "Bal KDD", and "Com Red KDD" depicted in Table 4.1.

First, the proposed hybrid sampling algorithm, HySCBA (detail in Section 2.8), is utilized to balance the class distribution of attack types (DoS, Probe, R2L and U2R) on multi-class imbalanced dataset "Atk Uni KDD". The obtained balanced dataset "Bal KDD" is shown in Table 4.1. Tables 2.17, 2.18 and 2.19 show that classifiers perform better when employed HySCBA except DoS attack. The reason is as it has significantly out numbers the number of instances of other classes (Probe, R2L and U2R) when no sampling algorithm is applied. Therefore, integrating HySCBA before classification process improves the performance of classifiers particularly for minority classes and able to efficiently classify rare classes. Further, four datasets are constructed from "Bal KDD" dataset as DoS-Vs-Rest, Probe-Vs-Rest, R2L-Vs-Rest, and U2R-Vs-Rest by applying OVR binarization technique shown in Table 4.2.

Subsequently, the proposed HyFSA (Section 2.6) has been employed to obtain class-specific feature subset for each binary-class that represents each attack class. The obtained 4 feature subsets, summarized in Table 4.19, are evaluated by classifiers NB and C4.5. The performance of feature subsets is tested in terms of TPR, FPR, TNR, GM, PRE, F1-S, ROC, PRE, TBM, ACC, ERR, and RMSE using 10-fold cross validation. The HyFSA is compared with methods CFS, CON, IG and GR and also with 41 features. The experimental results by classifiers NB and C4.5 using 41 features, feature sets obtained by CFS, CON, IG, GR and HyFSA for DoS-Vs-Rest are shown in Tables 4.21 and 4.22; for Probe-Vs-Rest are shown in Tables 4.23 and 4.24; for R2L-Vs-Rest are shown in Tables 4.25 and 4.26; and for U2R-Vs-Rest are shown in Tables 4.27 and 4.28 respectively. The result achieved by classifier NB on the reduced feature set obtained by HyFSA outperformed the methods CFS, CON, IG, GR and full dataset in all evaluation metrics. Whereas, classifier C4.5 performs near to equal to the methods CFS, CON, IG, GR and full dataset. But the results improve in terms of reduction in feature set and time taken to build model. The comparative graphs of performance for classifiers NB and C4.5 on Full Set, CFS, CON, IG, GR, and HyFSA for DoS-Vs-Rest, Probe-Vs-Rest, R2L-Vs-Rest, and U2R-Vs-Rest in terms of TPR, GM, PRE, ROC, PRC and ACC are shown in Figures 4.2, 4.5, 4.8, and 4.11; in terms of TBM are shown in Figures 4.3, 4.6, 4.9, and 4.12; in terms of FPR and ERR are shown in Figures 4.4, 4.7, 4.10, and 4.13 respectively. The final four feature subsets obtained are combined to obtain single feature subset for the detection of type of attack. The combined feature subset consists of 20 features {1, 2, 3, 4, 5, 6, 8, 13, 14, 16, 18, 22, 23, 29, 30, 34, 35, 36, 37, and 38} shown in Table 4.19. The resultant dataset is named as "Com Red KDD".

Table 4.21: Experimental results of NB of feature sets for DoS-Vs-Rest

Metrics	Feature Selection Method (# Feature)					
	Full Set (41)	CFS (8)	CON (5)	IG (9)	GR (18)	HyFSA (9)
TPR(%)	97.8	97.9	94.6	98.7	98.9	**99.2**
FPR(%)	2.4	2.7	3.4	3.0	2.6	**1.9**
TNR(%)	97.6	97.3	96.6	97.0	97.4	**98.1**
GM(%)	97.7	97.6	95.6	97.8	98.1	**98.6**
PRE(%)	97.9	97.9	95.3	98.7	98.9	**99.2**
F1-S(%)	97.8	97.9	94.8	98.7	98.9	**99.2**
ROC(%)	98.8	97.6	98.8	98.8	98.9	**99.1**
PRC(%)	98.7	97.8	99.0	98.8	99.0	**99.2**
TBM (sec)	0.15	0.02	0.02	0.03	0.05	0.03
ACC (%)	97.83	97.91	94.65	98.74	98.86	**99.20**
ERR (%)	2.17	2.09	5.35	1.26	1.14	**0.80**
RMSE(%)	14.59	14.12	20.96	11.19	10.60	**8.68**

Table 4.22: Experimental results of C4.5 of feature sets for DoS-Vs-Rest

Metrics	Feature Selection Method (# Feature)					
	Full Set (41)	CFS (8)	CON (5)	IG (9)	GR (18)	HyFSA (9)
TPR(%)	99.9	99.8	99.9	99.8	99.8	99.8
FPR(%)	0.2	0.3	0.2	0.4	0.5	0.6
TNR(%)	99.8	99.7	99.8	99.6	99.5	99.4
GM(%)	99.8	99.7	99.8	99.7	99.6	99.6
PRE(%)	99.9	99.8	99.9	99.8	99.8	99.8
F1-S(%)	99.9	99.8	99.9	99.8	99.8	99.8
ROC(%)	99.9	99.8	100.0	99.8	99.7	99.7
PRC(%)	99.9	99.8	100.0	99.8	99.7	99.8
TBM (sec)	1.31	0.3	0.06	0.19	0.27	**0.01**
ACC (%)	99.89	99.84	99.91	99.78	99.79	99.76
ERR (%)	0.12	0.16	0.10	0.22	0.21	0.24
RMSE(%)	3.33	3.96	3.05	4.49	4.52	4.88

Table 4.23: Experimental results of NB of feature sets for Probe-Vs-Rest

Metrics	Feature Selection Method (# Feature)					
	Full Set (41)	CFS (7)	CON (6)	IG (2)	GR (20)	HyFSA (6)
TPR(%)	80.4	71.6	84.5	97.5	94.4	**98.1**
FPR(%)	6.7	9.6	29.0	4.0	2.3	**2.3**
TNR(%)	93.3	90.4	71.0	96.0	97.7	**97.7**
GM(%)	86.6	80.5	77.5	96.7	96.0	**97.9**
PRE(%)	88.9	86.6	84.1	97.5	95.3	**98.2**
F1-S(%)	81.7	73.5	84.2	97.5	94.6	**98.1**
ROC(%)	98.5	99.1	81.5	98.7	99.4	99.3
PRC(%)	94.8	99.2	87.1	98.7	99.1	**99.2**
TBM (sec)	0.29	0.03	0.07	0.01	0.05	**0.01**
ACC (%)	80.43	71.63	84.50	97.47	94.43	**98.14**
ERR (%)	19.57	28.37	15.50	2.53	5.57	**1.86**
RMSE(%)	39.46	45.91	37.45	15.44	23.80	**14.15**

Table 4.24: Experimental results of C4.5 of feature sets for Probe-Vs-Rest

Metrics	Feature Selection Method (# Feature)					
	Full Set (41)	CFS (7)	CON (6)	IG (2)	GR (20)	HyFSA (6)
TPR(%)	99.9	99.3	99.7	98.9	99.9	99.7
FPR(%)	0.2	1.5	0.4	2.7	0.2	0.7
TNR(%)	99.8	98.5	99.6	97.3	99.8	99.3
GM(%)	99.8	98.9	99.6	98.1	99.8	99.5
PRE(%)	99.9	99.3	99.7	98.9	99.9	99.7
F1-S(%)	99.9	99.3	99.7	98.9	99.9	99.7
ROC(%)	99.9	99.9	99.7	98.8	99.9	99.8
PRC(%)	99.8	99.8	99.7	98.8	99.9	99.7
TBM (sec)	1.42	0.22	0.13	0.06	0.45	0.09
ACC (%)	99.91	99.34	99.73	98.90	99.90	99.71
ERR (%)	0.10	0.66	0.27	1.10	0.10	0.29
RMSE(%)	3.08	7.14	50.60	10.21	3.07	5.21

Table 4.25: Experimental results of NB of feature sets for R2L-Vs-Rest

Metrics	Feature Selection Method (# Feature)					
	Full Set (41)	CFS (5)	CON (7)	IG (34)	GR (26)	HyFSA (6)
TPR(%)	89.4	92.2	81.7	89.4	90.6	**93.2**
FPR(%)	5.7	13.5	53.2	5.7	5.0	12.1
TNR(%)	94.3	86.5	46.8	94.3	95.0	87.9
GM(%)	91.8	89.3	61.8	91.8	92.8	90.5
PRE(%)	91.9	92.2	83.6	91.9	92.6	**93.1**
F1-S(%)	89.9	92.2	77.9	89.9	91.0	**93.2**
ROC(%)	95.2	94.0	89.7	95.1	95.3	94.8
PRC(%)	94.2	94.4	90.5	94.2	94.4	**95.5**
TBM (sec)	0.13	0.02	0.02	0.1	0.07	0.03
ACC (%)	89.38	92.20	81.70	89.39	90.62	**93.18**
ERR (%)	10.62	7.80	18.30	10.61	9.38	**6.82**
RMSE(%)	32.28	27.07	42.67	32.25	29.80	**25.06**

Table 4.26: Experimental results of C4.5 of feature sets for R2L-Vs-Rest

Metrics	Feature Selection Method (# Feature)					
	Full Set (41)	CFS (5)	CON (7)	IG (34)	GR (26)	HyFSA (6)
TPR(%)	99.8	99.2	99.7	99.8	99.8	99.7
FPR(%)	0.5	1.9	0.7	0.5	0.5	0.7
TNR(%)	99.5	98.1	99.3	99.5	99.5	99.3
GM(%)	99.6	98.6	99.5	99.6	99.6	99.5
PRE(%)	99.8	99.2	99.7	99.8	99.8	99.7
F1-S(%)	99.8	99.2	99.7	99.8	99.8	99.7
ROC(%)	99.7	99.7	99.8	99.6	99.7	**99.8**
PRC(%)	99.6	99.7	99.8	99.6	99.7	**99.8**
TBM (sec)	1.2	0.09	0.15	0.78	0.53	**0.11**
ACC (%)	99.80	99.24	99.72	99.79	99.80	99.71
ERR (%)	0.20	0.76	0.28	0.21	0.20	0.29
RMSE(%)	4.53	8.36	5.27	4.58	4.44	5.40

Table 4.27: Experimental results of NB of feature sets for U2R-Vs-Rest

Metrics	Feature Selection Method (# Feature)					
	Full Set (41)	CFS (10)	CON (7)	IG (24)	GR (8)	HyFSA (9)
TPR(%)	83.9	77.8	51.4	83.8	92.8	**94.0**
FPR(%)	5.9	7.5	16.8	5.6	19.7	17.2
TNR(%)	94.1	92.5	83.2	94.4	80.3	82.8
GM(%)	88.9	84.8	65.4	88.9	86.3	88.2
PRE(%)	90.0	88.2	82.9	90.1	93.1	**94.3**
F1-S(%)	84.9	79.3	51.9	84.8	92.5	**93.7**
ROC(%)	93.6	98.1	94.7	95.2	94.8	**98.1**
PRC(%)	89.4	98.3	95.8	96.1	96.1	98.2
TBM (sec)	0.15	0.04	0.03	0.07	0.04	**0.02**
ACC (%)	83.92	77.82	51.43	83.83	92.82	**93.99**
ERR (%)	16.08	22.18	48.57	16.17	7.18	**6.01**
RMSE(%)	40.09	47.08	68.62	40.16	26.06	**21.83**

Table 4.28: Experimental results of C4.5 of feature sets for U2R-Vs-Rest

Metrics	Feature Selection Method (# Feature)					
	Full Set (41)	CFS (10)	CON (7)	IG (24)	GR (8)	HyFSA (9)
TPR(%)	99.9	99.5	99.8	99.8	99.4	99.6
FPR(%)	0.1	0.8	0.2	0.1	1.0	0.8
TNR(%)	99.9	99.2	99.8	99.9	99.0	99.2
GM(%)	99.9	99.3	99.8	99.8	99.2	99.4
PRE(%)	99.9	99.5	99.8	99.8	99.4	99.6
F1-S(%)	99.9	99.5	99.8	99.8	99.4	99.6
ROC(%)	99.9	99.4	99.9	99.9	99.3	99.4
PRC(%)	99.9	99.5	99.9	99.8	99.4	99.5
TBM (sec)	1.64	0.37	0.11	0.59	0.12	0.18
ACC (%)	99.87	99.50	99.83	99.82	99.42	99.63
ERR (%)	0.13	0.50	0.17	0.18	0.58	0.37
RMSE(%)	3.50	6.92	3.88	4.20	7.48	5.99

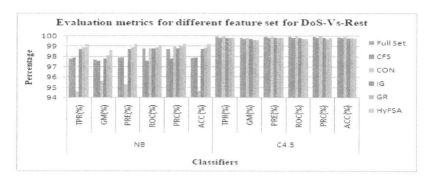

Figure 4.2: Comparison of TPR, GM, PRE, ROC, PRC & ACC for DoS-Vs-Rest

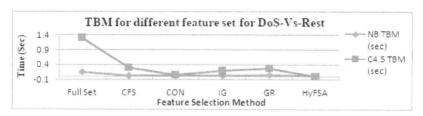

Figure 4.3: Comparison of TBM for DoS-Vs-Rest

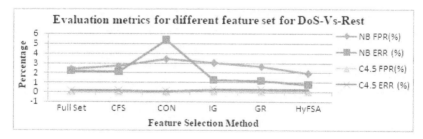

Figure 4.4: Comparison of FPR & ERR for DoS-Vs-Rest

In model development phase, OVR multi-class HEIC classifier is built on "Com Red KDD" dataset using 10-fold cross validation. This model represents Module II for the detection of attack type. Table 4.20 depicts the performance of OVR multi-class HEIC on different datasets "Atk Uni KDD", "Bal KDD" and "Com Red KDD" using 10-fold cross validation. Table 4.20 shows that proposed Module II built on reduced dataset "Com Red KDD" obtained same or better results than on

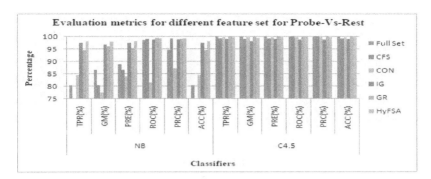

Figure 4.5: Comparison of TPR, GM, PRE, ROC, PRC & ACC for Probe-Vs-Rest

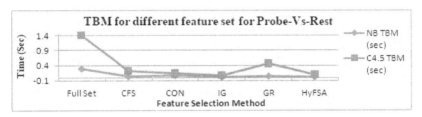

Figure 4.6: Comparison of TBM for Probe-Vs-Rest

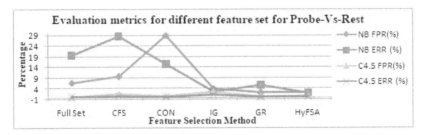

Figure 4.7: Comparison of FPR & ERR for Probe-Vs-Rest

full datasets "Atk Uni KDD" and "Bal KDD" in all performance evaluation metrics except PRE of U2R class, and F1-S of U2R and Probe classes. But they performed near to equal to the performance on "Bal KDD". The TBM is reduced by 80.12% from 257.15 sec to 51.12 sec.

The four single classifiers NB, C4.5, k-NN (k=3) and RIPPER are also built on

130

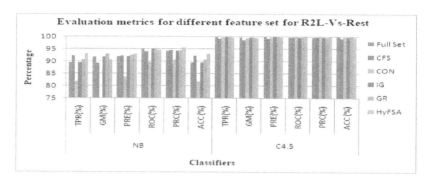

Figure 4.8: Comparison of TPR, GM, PRE, ROC, PRC & ACC for R2L-Vs-Rest

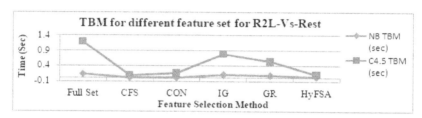

Figure 4.9: Comparison of TBM for R2L-Vs-Rest

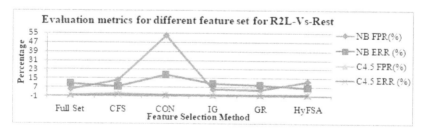

Figure 4.10: Comparison of FPR & ERR for R2L-Vs-Rest

datasets "Atk Uni KDD", "Bal KDD" and "Com Red KDD" using 10-fold cross validation for comparison. The results of the classifiers NB, C4.5, k-NN (k=3) and RIPPER are depicted in Tables 4.29, 4.30, 4.31, and 4.32 respectively. From Table 4.29, as can be seen that classifier NB obtained equal or superior performance on 41 features than reduced 20 features on all evaluation metrics except TBM; FPR and TNR of R2L; ROC of DoS and R2L; PRC of DoS, R2L and U2R. The TBM is

131

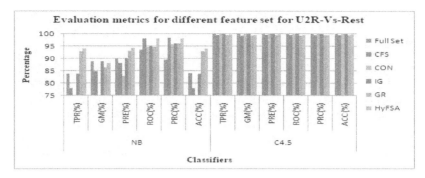

Figure 4.11: Comparison of TPR, GM, PRE, ROC, PRC & ACC for
U2R-Vs-Rest

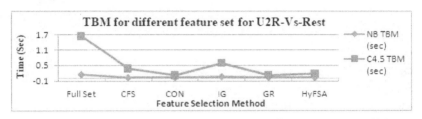

Figure 4.12: Comparison of TBM for U2R-Vs-Rest

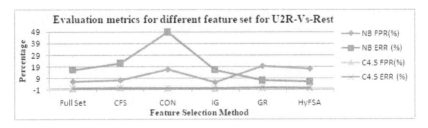

Figure 4.13: Comparison of FPR & ERR for U2R-Vs-Rest

reduced by 50% from 0.12 sec to 0.06 sec. Table 4.30 shows that C4.5 performed better on reduced 20 features in terms of TPR and F1-S of Probe; FPR, TNR, and GM of DoS. It has equal and near to equal performance on rest of the performance evaluation metrics. The TBM has reduced to 71.32% from 1.29 sec to 0.92 sec. It is evident from Table 4.31 that classifier k-NN (k=3) obtained same or better results employing reduced dataset "Com Red KDD" than "Atk Uni KDD" and "Bal

KDD" except FPR, TNR and PRE of U2R; F1-S of Probe. The classifier RIPPER also performed better on reduced dataset "Com Red KDD" than "Atk Uni KDD" and "Bal KDD" except TBM; PRE, FI-S and PRC of DoS; TPR of R2L; TPR, FPR, TNR, GM, and F1-S of U2R. The TBM has reduced to 60% from 7.87 sec to 4.72 sec. As can be seen from Tables 4.29, 4.30, 4.31, and 4.32, TBM for 41 features are remarkably higher than reduced 20 features. The TBM is decreased by approximately 50-80% except for kNN.

The comparison of Module II with classifiers NB, C4.5, k-NN (k=3) and RIPPER on "Com Red KDD" using 10-fold cross validation using performance evaluation metrics TPR, FPR, TNR, GM, TBM, PRE, FI-S, ROC and PRC is summarized in Table 4.33. From Table 4.33, the proposed model of Module II outperformed classifiers NB, C4.5, k-NN (k=3) and RIPPER on reduced dataset "Com Red KDD" on all performance evaluation metrics except FPR, TNR, PRE and F1-S of Probe; TPR of R2L; PRE of U2R.

On the comparison of results of 4 classifiers (Tables 4.29 to 4.32) and OVR multi-class HEIC for Module II (Table 4.20) based on TPR, FPR, TNR, GM, TBM, PRE, FI-S, ROC and PRC on datasets "Atk Uni KDD", "Bal KDD" and "Com Red KDD" has shown that OVR multi-class HEIC for Module II on reduced 20 features set ("Com Red KDD") outperformed other classifiers on datasets ("Atk Uni KDD", "Bal KDD" and "Com Red KDD") and hence more capable and reliable for NIDS and therefore selected as model for Module II.

Table 4.29: Experimental results of NB on different datasets

Metrics	Attack Name	Dataset (# Feature)		
		Atk Uni KDD (41)	Bal KDD(41)	Com Red KDD (20)
TPR	U2R	90.4	99.3	86.7
	DoS	96.2	99.5	96.1
	R2L	36.7	42.3	29.5
	Probe	91.8	99.7	99.4
FPR	U2R	2.0	18.8	17.1
	DoS	0.3	0.2	1.1
	R2L	0.9	0.6	0.5
	Probe	2.4	2.4	10.7

Continue ...

Table 4.29 – (*Continued*)

Metrics	Attack	Dataset (# Feature)		
	Name	Atk Uni KDD (41)	Bal KDD(41)	Com Red KDD (20)
TNR	U2R	98.0	81.2	82.9
	DoS	99.7	99.8	98.9
	R2L	99.1	99.4	99.5
	Probe	97.6	97.6	89.3
GM	U2R	94.1	89.8	84.8
	DoS	97.9	99.6	97.5
	R2L	60.3	64.8	54.2
	Probe	94.7	98.6	94.2
TBM (Sec.)	-	0.34	0.12	0.06
PRE	U2R	3.7	63.0	62.8
	DoS	100.0	99.3	96.7
	R2L	42.9	96.1	94.9
	Probe	73.8	93.3	75.7
F1-S	U2R	7.1	76.2	72.9
	DoS	98.1	97.4	96.4
	R2L	39.5	58.8	45.1
	Probe	81.8	96.4	85.9
ROC	U2R	99.3	96.7	96.8
	DoS	99.6	99.0	99.4
	R2L	98.8	96.9	97.3
	Probe	97.9	99.6	99.2
PRC	U2R	22.3	92.3	92.6
	DoS	100.0	98.3	98.9
	R2L	57.9	89.2	91.1
	Probe	78.1	99.7	96.3

Table 4.30: Experimental results of C4.5 on different datasets

Metrics	Attack	Dataset (# Feature)		
	Name	Atk Uni KDD (41)	Bal KDD (41)	Com Red KDD (20)
TPR	U2R	82.7	99.8	99.7
	DoS	100.0	99.8	99.8

Continue . . .

Table 4.30 – (*Continued*)

Metrics	Attack Name	Dataset (# Feature)		
		Atk Uni KDD (41)	Bal KDD (41)	Com Red KDD (20)
	R2L	98.2	99.6	99.4
	Probe	99.7	99.7	99.8
FPR	U2R	0.0	0.1	0.2
	DoS	0.5	0.1	0.0
	R2L	0.0	0.1	0.1
	Probe	0.0	0.1	0.1
TNR	U2R	100.0	99.9	99.8
	DoS	99.5	99.9	100.0
	R2L	100.0	99.9	99.9
	Probe	100.0	99.9	99.9
GM	U2R	90.9	99.8	99.7
	DoS	99.7	99.8	99.9
	R2L	99.1	99.7	99.6
	Probe	99.8	99.8	99.8
TBM (Sec.)	-	4.76	1.29	0.92
PRE	U2R	79.6	99.6	99.5
	DoS	100.0	99.8	99.9
	R2L	99.4	99.8	99.7
	Probe	99.6	99.7	99.7
F1-S	U2R	81.1	99.7	99.6
	DoS	100.0	99.8	99.8
	R2L	98.8	99.7	99.6
	Probe	99.6	99.7	99.8
ROC	U2R	95.0	99.9	99.8
	DoS	99.9	100.0	99.9
	R2L	99.4	99.8	99.7
	Probe	99.8	99.9	99.9
PRC	U2R	68.0	99.4	99.4
	DoS	100.0	99.9	99.8
	R2L	98.7	99.7	99.2
	Probe	99.6	99.6	99.6

135

Table 4.31: Experimental results of k-NN (k=3) on different datasets

Metrics	Attack Name	Dataset (# Feature)		
		Atk Uni KDD (41)	Bal KDD (41)	Com Red KDD (20)
TPR	U2R	71.2	99.5	99.7
	DoS	100.0	99.9	99.9
	R2L	98.8	99.3	99.3
	Probe	99.8	99.8	99.8
FPR	U2R	0.0	0.2	0.3
	DoS	0.2	0.0	0.0
	R2L	0.0	0.2	0.1
	Probe	0.0	0.0	0.0
TNR	U2R	100.0	99.8	99.7
	DoS	99.8	100.0	100.0
	R2L	100.0	99.8	99.9
	Probe	100.0	100.0	100.0
GM	U2R	84.4	99.6	99.7
	DoS	99.9	99.9	99.9
	R2L	99.4	99.5	99.6
	Probe	99.9	99.9	99.9
TBM (Sec.)	-	0.01	0.01	0.01
PRE	U2R	80.4	99.3	99.2
	DoS	100.0	99.9	99.9
	R2L	98.8	99.5	99.7
	Probe	99.8	99.9	99.9
F1-S	U2R	75.5	99.4	99.5
	DoS	100.0	99.9	99.9
	R2L	98.8	99.4	99.5
	Probe	99.8	99.9	99.8
ROC	U2R	91.9	99.8	99.9
	DoS	100.0	100.0	100.0
	R2L	99.9	99.8	99.8
	Probe	100.0	99.9	99.9
PRC	U2R	81.6	99.4	99.4
	DoS	100.0	99.9	99.9

Continue ...

Table 4.31 – (*Continued*)

Metrics	Attack Name	Dataset (# Feature)		
		Atk Uni KDD (41)	Bal KDD (41)	Com Red KDD (20)
	R2L	98.6	99.5	99.6
	Probe	99.9	99.9	99.9

Table 4.32: Experimental results of RIPPER on different datasets

Metrics	Attack Name	Dataset (# Feature)		
		Atk Uni KDD (41)	Bal KDD (41)	Com Red KDD (20)
TPR	U2R	90.4	99.9	99.8
	DoS	100.0	100.0	100.0
	R2L	98.6	99.6	99.7
	Probe	99.7	99.9	99.8
FPR	U2R	0.0	0.1	0.1
	DoS	0.3	0.0	0.0
	R2L	0.0	0.0	0.0
	Probe	0.0	0.1	0.0
TNR	U2R	100.0	99.9	99.9
	DoS	99.7	100.0	100.0
	R2L	100.0	100.0	100.0
	Probe	100.0	99.9	100.0
GM	U2R	95.1	99.9	99.8
	DoS	99.8	100.0	100.0
	R2L	99.3	99.8	99.8
	Probe	99.8	99.9	99.9
TBM (Sec.)		23.76	7.87	4.72
PRE	U2R	75.8	99.7	99.7
	DoS	100.0	99.9	99.9
	R2L	99.6	99.9	99.9
	Probe	99.7	99.8	99.9
F1-S	U2R	82.5	99.8	99.7
	DoS	100.0	99.9	99.9
	R2L	98.6	99.7	99.8
	Probe	99.7	99.8	99.9

Continue ...

Table 4.32 – (*Continued*)

Metrics	Attack Name	Dataset (# Feature)		
		Atk Uni KDD (41)	Bal KDD (41)	Com Red KDD (20)
ROC	U2R	95.3	99.9	99.9
	DoS	99.8	100.0	100.0
	R2L	99.7	99.8	99.9
	Probe	99.8	99.9	99.9
PRC	U2R	68.2	99.6	99.7
	DoS	100.0	99.9	99.9
	R2L	99.0	99.7	99.8
	Probe	99.6	99.8	99.8

Table 4.33: Experimental results of NB, C4.5, k-NN (k=3), RIPPER & Module II on "Com Red KDD"

Metrics	Attack Name	Classifiers				
		NB-SGD	C4.5	k-NN (k=3)	RIPPER	Module II
TPR	U2R	86.7	99.7	99.7	99.8	100.0
	DoS	96.1	99.8	99.9	100.0	100.0
	R2L	29.5	99.4	99.3	99.7	99.6
	Probe	99.4	99.8	99.8	99.8	99.9
FPR	U2R	17.1	0.2	0.3	0.1	0.1
	DoS	1.1	0.0	0.0	0.0	0.0
	R2L	0.5	0.1	0.1	0.0	0.0
	Probe	10.7	0.1	0.0	0.0	0.1
TNR	U2R	82.9	99.8	99.7	99.9	99.9
	DoS	98.9	100.0	100.0	100.0	100.0
	R2L	99.5	99.9	99.9	100.0	100.0
	Probe	89.3	99.9	100.0	100.0	99.9
GM	U2R	84.8	99.7	99.7	99.8	99.9
	DoS	97.5	99.9	99.9	100.0	100.0
	R2L	54.2	99.6	99.6	99.8	99.8
	Probe	94.2	99.8	99.9	99.9	99.9
TBM (Sec.)	-	0.06	0.92	0.01	4.72	51.12
PRE	U2R	62.8	99.5	99.2	99.7	99.6
	DoS	96.7	99.9	99.9	99.9	100.0

Continue ...

Table 4.33 – (*Continued*)

Metrics	Attack Name	Classifiers				
		NB-SGD	C4.5	k-NN (k=3)	RIPPER	Module II
	R2L	94.9	99.7	99.7	99.9	100.0
	Probe	75.7	99.7	99.9	99.9	99.8
F1-S	U2R	72.9	99.6	99.5	99.7	99.8
	DoS	96.4	99.8	99.9	99.9	100.0
	R2L	45.1	99.6	99.5	99.8	99.8
	Probe	85.9	99.8	99.8	99.9	99.8
ROC	U2R	96.8	99.8	99.9	99.9	100.0
	DoS	99.4	99.9	100.0	100.0	100.0
	R2L	97.3	99.7	99.8	99.9	99.9
	Probe	99.2	99.9	99.9	99.9	100.0
PRC	U2R	92.6	99.4	99.4	99.7	99.9
	DoS	98.9	99.8	99.9	99.9	100.0
	R2L	91.1	99.2	99.6	99.8	99.9
	Probe	96.3	99.6	99.9	99.8	100.0

The comparative graphs for the performance of classifiers NB, C4.5, k-NN (n=3), RIPPER and proposed Module II in terms of GM, PRE, F1-S and PRC on datasets "Atk Uni KDD", "Bal KDD", and "Com Red KDD" are shown in Figures 4.14 to 4.18 respectively. The comparative graph for the performance comparison of individual classifiers NB, C4.5, k-NN (k=3), RIPPER, and Module II in terms of GM, PRE, F1-S and PRC on reduced dataset "Com Red KDD" is shown in Figure 4.19 and in terms of TBM on datasets "Atk Uni KDD", "Bal KDD", and "Com Red KDD" is shown in Figure 4.20. The results strongly indicate that by employing sampling technique, separate feature set for each attack type and OVR multi-class HEIC classifier improves the performance of all attack classes equally (both majority and minority class) and has faster TBM than the full features set.

4.5 SUMMARY

This chapter presented the methodology for Module II, which is a part of proposed NIDPS presented in Section 2.3. The purpose of Module II to detect the type of attack with the aim to enhance the accuracy and efficiency of the system as well

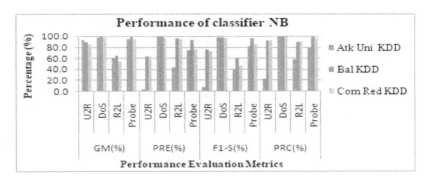

Figure 4.14: GM, PRE, F1-S & PRC of NB

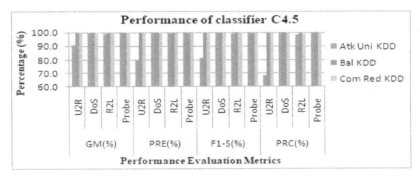

Figure 4.15: GM, PRE, F1-S & PRC of C4.5

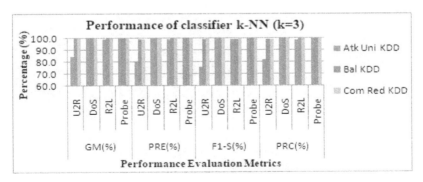

Figure 4.16: GM, PRE, F1-S & PRC of k-NN

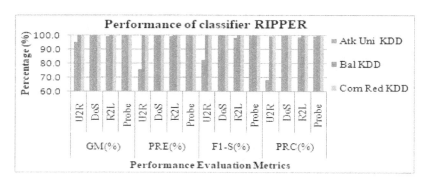

Figure 4.17: GM, PRE, F1-S & PRC of RIPPER

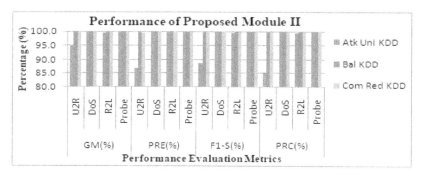

Figure 4.18: GM, PRE, F1-S & PRC of Module II

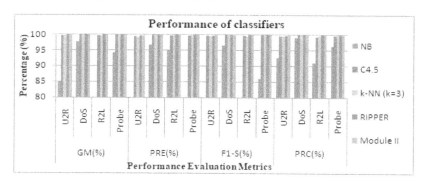

Figure 4.19: GM, PRE, F1-S & PRC of classifiers on Com Red KDD

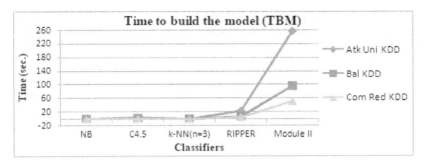

Figure 4.20: TBM (in sec.) of classifiers

as reduce the FPR, ERR, and TBM of the classifier. The main challenging issues arise in IDS are to handle large-scale high dimensional multi-class imbalanced
dataset and maximizing overall ACC and minimizing FPR and ERR for all classes.
The Module II addresses these issues by incorporating hybrid sampling algorithm
HySCBA to overcome class imbalance problem, OVR binarization technique, feature selection approach HyFSA to obtain class specific feature set for each attack
type, and OVR multi-class HEIC classifier. The results showed that the performance of Module II has been improved in terms of TPR, TNR, GM, PRE, F1-S,
ROC, and PRC with minimum FPR and computation time for all attack classes
(both majority and minority class).

* * * * *

AN INTELLIGENT ENSEMBLE BASED SYSTEM FOR DETECTING AND COMBATING INTRUSION IN COMPUTER NETWORK

A THESIS

Submitted by

AMRITA

In partial fulfillment for the award of the degree of

DOCTOR OF PHILOSOPHY

in

COMPUTER SCIENCE AND ENGINEERING

Under the supervision of

Dr. Shri Kant

**Department of Computer Science and Engineering,
Sharda Univerity, Greater Noida**

SCHOOL OF ENGINEERING AND TECHNOLOGY
SHARDA UNIVERSITY, GREATER NOIDA-201310

JULY - 2019

CHAPTER 5

CONCLUSION AND FUTURE SCOPE OF RESEARCH

5.1 INTRODUCTION

This chapter provides the overall idea about this research work. In this work, an anomaly based NIDPS is proposed to defeat the limitations of the existing IDSs (detail in Chapter 2). The proposed system consists of three modules—(i) Module I: Methodology for NIDS to detect normal or attack traffic, (ii) Module II: Methodology for NIDS to detect specific attack type, and (iii) Module III: Methodology for IPS to prevent from identified attack traffic. The detail of modules Module I, Module II and Module III are presented in Chapter 3, Chapter 4 and Chapter 2 respectively. The next section presents the summary of the research work carried out in the previous chapters. The future research work is discussed in the last section.

5.2 SUMMARY OF THE RESEARCH WORK

The purpose of this section is to summarize the main achievements of this research work in terms of aim and objectives. The aim was **"to create a lightweight, accurate, efficient and intelligent Intrusion Detection and Prevention System for Computer Network(s) Security"**. To achieve this aim, following objectives were set:

Objective 1: To propose an intelligent model for NIDS that is accurate (high DR and low FAR) and lightweight to detect intrusion (attack) from network traffic in real time.

Objective 2: To propose an intelligent model for NIDS that is accurate and lightweight to further identify attack types from intrusion in network traffic in real time.

Objective 3: To propose a model to combat from intrusion once it is detected.

Objective 4: To identify appropriate evaluation metrics to measure the performance of proposed model.

To achieve the aim, an anomaly-based NIDPS was proposed in Chapter 2. The Objectives 1, 2, and 3 are accomplished by Module I presented in Chapter 3, Module II presented in Chapter 4, and Module III presented in Section 2.3.4 of Chapter 2 respectively. The Objective 4 is presented in Section 2.4 of Chapter 2. The contributions of this research are summarized chapter wise as follows:

Chapter 1 presents overview, introduction about IDPS, and the literature review related to anomaly-based NIDPS carried out for this research work, the motivation, research question, aim and objectives, research contributions and novelty of this thesis work and organization of the thesis. The literature review carried out on different techniques applied to anomaly-based NIDS using single classifier, ensemble and hybrid classifiers, feature selection and classification for multiple class imbalanced dataset employing feature selection approaches and IPS.

Chapter 2 discusses in detail the foundations of the methods / topics used in this research. It includes feature selection methods, single classifier, ensemble of classifiers, and methods for combating class imbalanced problem in multi-class case. After this, the chapter discusses the system architecture design of research work for anomaly based NIDPS. For this research work, the system architecture is modeled and designed with the three major modules— (i) Module I: Methodology for NIDS to detect normal or attack traffic, (ii) Module II: Methodology for NIDS to detect specific attack type, and (iii) Module III: Methodology for IPS to prevent from identified attack traffic. Then the chapter describes in details the evaluation metrics used to evaluate the proposed work and detail of the datasets (KDD-Cup-1999 and NSL-KDD) used in the experiments. Further, the chapter discusses the detail of proposed hybrid feature selection approach (HyFSA). The proposed HyFSA is capable of obtaining optimal number of features and maximize the ACC, minimize the FPR, TBM, and TTM of the system in which it is being used. This method is useful in any domain in which there is a need of feature selection method. For the present work, it has been used to obtain following:

- optimal number of features for normal and attack classification
- different sets of optimal number of features for each type of attacks (DoS, Probe, R2L and U2R) from imbalanced multi-class dataset instead of one set of features for all attack types

The proposed HEIC is presented next to overcome the limitation of single classifier to detect intrusion from the incoming traffic at an early stage and further identify the type of intrusions in detected intrusive network traffic in real time using selected features by HyFSA. The proposed hybrid sampling algorithm for multi-class imbalanced dataset, HySCBA, is presented in the last section. This algorithm is a combination of under-sampling and over-sampling techniques to handle the class imbalance of attack types in dataset. The algorithm, experimental setup, and experimental results and analysis are discussed for all proposed algorithms.

Chapter 3 provides the methodology for Module I (HyFSA-HEIC) for intelligent lightweight, accurate, and efficient anomaly based NIDS, which is a part of proposed NIDPS. The chapter presents block diagram of Module I (HyFSA-HEIC), the experimental setup, and experimental result and analysis. The purpose of this module is to detect whether the incoming network traffic is normal or attack. The main challenging issues arise in IDS are to handle high dimensional large dataset and maximizing overall ACC and less false alarm. The Module I (HyFSA-HEIC) addresses these issues by incorporating HyFSA and HEIC. It utilized 5 classifiers NB, NN-SGD, RIPPER, DT (C4.5) and RF and Majority Voting to produce the final decisions of these 5 classifiers using only 6 features i.e. only 15% of original 41 features. The results showed that Module I (HyFSA-HEIC) outperformed other methods in terms of TPR (99.9%), ACC (99.91%), PRE (99.9%), ROC (99.9%), and low FPR (0.1%) and RMSE (3.06%) using only 6 features. It also reduced the TMB by 50.79% and TTM by 55.30%.

Chapter 4 discusses the methodology for Module II for intelligent lightweight, accurate, and efficient anomaly based NIDS, which is a part of proposed NIDPS. The purpose of this module is to detect type of attack, once attack is detected in incoming network traffic. The main challenging issues arise in IDS are to handle high dimensional large multi-class imbalanced dataset and maximizing overall ACC and minimizing FPR and ERR for all classes. The Module II addresses these issues by incorporating hybrid sampling algorithm HySCBA to overcome class imbalance problem, OVR binarization technique, feature selection approach HyFSA to obtain class specific feature set for each attack type, and OVR multi-class HEIC classifier. The results showed that the performance of Module II has been improved in terms of TPR, TNR, GM, PRE, F1-S, ROC, and PRC with minimum FPR and computation time for all attack classes (both majority and minority class).

5.3   FUTURE SCOPE OF RESEARCH

In future, it is possible to provide extensions or modifications to the proposed methodology using more robust intelligent agents or other more robust intelligent paradiam to achieve further increased performance and to improve the detection accuracy and to reduce the FNR and FPR.

The Internet of Things (IoT) has emerged as new paradigm. It has ability to integrate physical objects and the Internet, which helps to create smart environments. The privacy and security have become an important issue and essential component in IoT environments. Also IoT devices has limited storage capabilities and computing power. Therefore, the work can be extented for:

- To strengthen the technique for IPS for better IDPS.

- IDS / IPS development for resource constraint devices and sensor network.

- IDS / IPS development for IoT network.

* * * * *

CPSIA information can be obtained
at www.ICGtesting.com
Printed in the USA
BVHW060854140123
656278BV00011B/1550